Making Scenes 3
Short Plays for Young Actors

Indian Summer by Harwant Bains, **Almost Grown** by Richard Ca......ce
Palace by Lucinda Coxon (adapted from the novel by Tarjei Vesaas), **The Dark Tower** by Louis MacNeice

Making Scenes 3 is an anthology of four short plays for young actors performed across Britain and showcased at the Royal National Theatre in June and July 1995, as part of the BT National Connections festival.

Each play is accompanied by an interview with its author by Jim Mulligan; acting notes and exercises for young actors by Suzy Graham-Adriani, Director/Producer for BT National Connections; and the volume is introduced by Literary Consultant Nick Drake.

BT is proud to sponsor BT National Connections, an Education Project of the Royal National Theatre, providing over 4000 young people with the unique opportunity of working on new plays and translations specially commissioned or selected from a group of recognized playwrights.

It is through projects such as these that BT is able to help bring the enjoyment and benefits of the arts to communities throughout the UK. Rodger Broad, BT's Head of Corporate Sponsorship said, 'It is not often that a company is offered the opportunity to help develop and then sponsor a project that so completely supports its own objectives of "adding to the quality of life in the communities in which it conducts its business". In BT National Connections, we have found the perfect project to do just that.'

Making Scenes 3

Short Plays for Young Actors

Indian Summer
Harwant Bains

Almost Grown
Richard Cameron

The Ice Palace
Lucinda Coxon
*(adapted from the novel by Tarjei Vesaas, translated from
the Norwegian by Elizabeth Rokkan)*

The Dark Tower
Louis MacNeice

*Introduced by Nick Drake,
with author interviews by Jim Mulligan
and production notes by Suzy Graham-Adriani*

**Methuen Drama
in association with the Royal National Theatre**

Methuen New Theatrescripts
in association with the Royal National Theatre

First published in Great Britain 1995
by Methuen Drama in association with the Royal National Theatre
an imprint of Reed Consumer Books Ltd
Michelin House, 81 Fulham Road, London SW3 6RB
and Auckland, Melbourne, Singapore and Toronto

ISBN 0 413 69860 2

A CIP catalogue record for this book is available at the British Library

Front cover image courtesy of Tony Stone Images

Typeset by Wilmaset Ltd, Birkenhead, Wirral
Printed by Clays Ltd, St Ives plc

Contents

BT National Connections

The plays, introduced by **Nick Drake**, *the scheme's Literary Consultant*

'As the guardians of public morals warned, youngsters are enacting scenes from Quentin Tarantino's *Pulp Fiction*. However, the results were not the violence that had been predicted. Last week, there were reports of two sixteen-year-old pupils at a comprehensive near Bristol performing the opening "Pumpkin/Honey-Bunny" scenes from *Pulp Fiction* for a mock GCSE drama exam. The two dismissed classical choices such as *Twelfth Night* and *Pygmalion*, and won a borderline A grade for their performance.' *Screen*, March 1995.

There are at least three points to be made from this news item; firstly, there's a hunger for new plays among young actors; secondly, there's a poverty of original plays by exceptional writers available to them; and thirdly, young people are excited by writing which is absolutely contemporary, sophisticated, and preferably heretical in its use of form and language. At the same time, playwrights – especially new playwrights – have found the opportunities for productions of their new work diminishing around the country: most theatres' repertoires are now filled largely with revivals, productions of old plays by long-dead writers, and adaptations of novels.

Suzy Graham-Adriani and the Royal National Theatre had been researching ways of answering these needs, and she and I began to discuss how to turn the situation into a creative opportunity. Put simply, we wanted to create an exciting and innovative repertoire of new plays by important playwrights for young actors to perform principally for audiences of their peers. In March 1994, with the National's backing, we began to ask playwrights whose work we admired if they would be interested in the idea; the plays would be produced not once, but many times in different venues, and with different ideas and interpretations, all around the country; there would be regional festivals at ten partnership theatres, and the whole scheme would culminate with a big festival of ten productions at the Royal National Theatre in London in June and July 1995. Thanks to generous sponsorship from BT, we were able to bring this whole concept to life in a project called 'BT National Connections'.

We explained to the writers that the plays could only be about an hour long, but that otherwise they were free to write about whatever interested them (as they absolutely ought to be), and for as big a cast as they wished. We commissioned six new plays, two translations of interesting and relatively unknown works (one of which – *The Ice Palace* – was adapted from a short Norwegian novel), and included two new plays that had already been written, but which had not had proper productions, and which were then worked on further by the writers. And I found two older, but remarkable and little-known plays; this made up a portfolio of twelve.

The writers began work in the spring of 1994, and produced first drafts that September. The first reading of these drafts was incredibly exciting; brand new work from important writers. Each play was unexpected, original and above all a work of the imagination; vivid language, big stories, fascinating characters; in each there was a various, and large-hearted sense that the world was bigger and stranger than you had thought. There were plays set in difficult urban worlds, in a clearing in a wood, in a remote village in winter; plays about love, about freedom, and above all about journeys. And however obliquely, they all discovered original theatrical ways of looking at the world *now*.

The plays were completed in November and early December 1994. We circulated descriptions of the writers and the plays to all the groups involved in the scheme, and then invited representatives of each group to come to the National for a day of workshops with the writers on their plays, led by accomplished directors of new writing. As I write this, there are one hundred and fifty productions of these plays in rehearsal in every part of the land. And the publication of the plays in these volumes means that they are now available to anyone to discover for themselves. They constitute the first plays in a new repertoire of new writing.

The Plays: Volume Three

The Ice Palace is set in a remote village in winter. Two girls, Siss and Unn, strike up an immediate and intense friendship. They look into a mirror; Unn shares her terrible secret; Siss is deeply shocked. Then Unn suddenly disappears – all in the first ten pages. The play dramatises the unexpected and inexplicable *suddenness* of events and emotions in life, and explores how Unn's vanishing precipitates enormous and far-reaching changes in Siss's life. Siss's journey is a big emotional and dramatic arc, which takes her from despair to a kind of realisation about life and death, a discovery of forgiveness, and an understanding that the living have a right to go on living. The play also explores the power of the imagination to recreate the world in stories and poetry. Its dramatic landscapes create a thunderous sense of both the magical grace and the imminent danger of the world; as the class make up a story about the world around them, Unn actually explores it; Unn tells Siss her terrible secret, in a few words made as potent as a spell or a curse; and Siss must keep that secret for as long as she can bear – until she can tell it, and free herself from its burden.

Almost Grown is also set in a small town, this time in South Yorkshire; but its detailed, specific world carries resonances that echo far into the hinterlands of the emotions. Moving backwards and forwards in time, the play traces the history and the consequences of a tragic accident among a once close-knit group of friends. We see Dave, Scott and Tommy when they're still in their early teens, and also when they're in their early twenties, having left school, gone their very different ways, and met up again; time enough for us and them to sense the gap between who they were and what they dreamed of becoming when they were kids, and who and what they are now. In between, Elaine, Dave's sister, has been knocked down in a hit-and-run accident, and is in a coma. No one knows who was driving the car that knocked her down, or who was the passenger. Violence, guilt, and the need for some kind of redemption from both, haunt the characters in different ways, until the confession of the truth becomes a terrible and necessary final confrontation.

Indian Summer also looks back into the past; in this case a small town in India in the 1960s. Kulwant, born in London of Indian parents, is visiting India with his mother. He is befriended by Titoo, a local kid who is desperate to leave India; they fly kites from rooftops, eat tutti-frutti ice-cream (it's the only available flavour), and taunt a Holy Man who has sat in the street for years with a sword through his mouth: an act of remembrance of God, as he puts it. When Kulwant, encouraged by Titoo, pulls out the sword, a remarkable and frank friendship is established between the mystic and the boy. Like many of Harwant Bains's plays, *Indian Summer* is concerned with the predicament of exile, and uses the rich, difficult, and sometimes surreal dislocations and displacements between the cultures of the East and West to create its dramatic world. Kulwant is taken back to where home ought to be – but it isn't there. This confronts him with his own oddity, the ambiguity of his identity, and the unreliability of his assumptions about the world. 'East, West, home's best' is the saying; but where is 'home' for him when he finds himself caught between the two worlds, and belongs in his own heart to neither? Neither India, with its heat, chattering relatives, holy men and fighting kites, nor back in cold and rainy London where he was born. Even the Holy Man, with his insight, has no answer to that question.

The Dark Tower was written as a radio play, and broadcast on the BBC Home Service in January 1946. Much of its imagery of ghost towns, ruins, and 'deserts of dried-up hopes', and its dispossessed, sometimes ghostly characters, were drawn from the devastation and chaos of the war. But the play was also inspired by a poem, Browning's nightmare ballad 'Childe Roland to the Dark Tower Came'. MacNeice wrote that the poem 'does not admit of a completely rational analysis and still less adds up to any clear moral or message. This poem has the solidity of a dream.' He also described *The Dark Tower* as 'a parable play' and compared it, in that sense, to *The Pilgrim's Progress* and Ibsen's *Peer Gynt*. Like those works, the play is a dream poem about a vision quest. Roland, the central character and trainee knight in arms, must undertake a journey which will test and validate his 'honour'; it has been prefigured as his family's ancient destiny to fight the Dark Tower. But as the Tutor tells him, no one has ever returned to describe the Tower; it is 'dark, and is the source / of Evil through the world. It is immortal / but men must try to kill it – and keep on trying / so long as we would be human.' As his quest continues through half-truths, hallucinations, doubts and riddles, he questions all the values he has been taught, and finds himself only approaching closer to the mysterious heart of his own fear, which he must finally confront.

March 1995

Indian Summer

Harwant Bains

Act One

Scene One

Flying a Kite On The Rooftop.

The roof-top of a house in a medium-sized Indian city. **Kulwant***, a boy of about ten, is watching an older boy* **Titoo***, who is about fourteen, flying a kite.* **Kulwant** *is wearing a floppy old straw hat, which is rather large for him.*

There are two other children, a boy and a girl, **Nita***, also sitting to one side playing marbles – the* **Boy** *is about six,* **Nita** *eleven.*

Titoo   Can I ask you one thing?

Kulwant   All right.

Titoo   Why are you wearing that big hat?

Beat.

Kulwant   My mum told me to. She doesn't want me getting burned out in the sun.

Titoo   Oh.

Beat.

I suppose you're not used to it like we are.

Kulwant   I only wear it 'cause she told me to. I don't need it. I'm used to the sun now.

Titoo   Did you come in the jet aeroplane?

Kulwant   No, we rowed a boat.

Titoo *throws him a look.*

Titoo   How come you speak Punjabi so good?

Kulwant   Mum and dad always speak it. When grandma came to stay with us I had to speak it with her all the time. Actually I had to shout it 'cause she's so deaf.

Short pause.

Titoo   She told everybody when she came back she didn't like England one bit. Too cold for her bones.

Beat.

You see how high it's going? You see? She caught some air rising.

Kulwant   Yes, I can see.

Beat. Authoritatively.

Warm air rises.

Titoo   Then how come we're not all floating around right now?

Beat.

You ever see a kite fly that high, eh? You ever seen that in England?

Kulwant   No.

Titoo   You ever flown a kite before?

Kulwant   No.

Beat.

Can you give me a go?

Titoo   Your mummy said not to. This string is sharp, you know, it's got glass on it.

Kulwant   Why?

Titoo   You don't know about how we fight kites?

Kulwant   No.

Titoo   Well, you wait, you keep your kite in the sky – you keep it there to invite other kite flyers to your piece of the sky. Pretty soon some boy will see this kite, so he'll climb up onto the roof of his house and launch his own. He'll fly closer and closer, I'll pull mine in a bit so I have plenty of string spare. Then, when the kites are almost next to each other, we cross strings. Like swords.

Kulwant   What happens?

Titoo   You let out the string fast as you can. One or the other will be cut. The better string, the better kite, the better flyer – that one will win. Sometimes you can spend a day and a night up on the roof fighting a good flyer.

Kulwant   A day and a night?

Titoo   Sometimes.

Kulwant   How can you see the kite in the dark?

Titoo   You don't have to see it. You just know where it is. It speaks to you.

Kulwant   How?

Beat.

Titoo   On the telephone.

Titoo *smiles. He hands the string to* **Kulwant**.
Carefully.

Kulwant   What do I do?

Titoo   Let it out gently.

Kulwant *starts to let out the string on the kite – it runs through his fingers.*

Kulwant   Shit!

Titoo   (*taking the string back from him*) I told you it was sharp!

Kulwant   It's bleeding!

Titoo   Now your mum's going to shout at me!

Kulwant *looks at* **Titoo**.

Kulwant   I won't tell her.

Titoo   What if she sees it bleeding?

Kulwant   She won't. I won't let her.

Long beat.

Titoo   Okay. It's just she'd get me into trouble with the old man. He'd beat the shit out of me.

Kulwant   Would he?

Titoo   Doesn't your dad?

Kulwant   No.

Titoo   Not even when he's angry as hell?

Kulwant   No.

Pause.

He hit my mum once.

Titoo   Mine does that too. But my mum hits him back harder. What's your mum do?

Kulwant   Nothing. They had a big row. It was just before we came here.

Titoo   Your dad didn't come?

Kulwant   No. Mum said he couldn't get a holiday from the factory.

Titoo   You going to see him again?

Kulwant   Course I am – when we go back.

Short pause.

Titoo You've come to live here though, haven't you – forever?

Kulwant No way!

Titoo I heard your mum talking to some of the women. She's saying she's gonna put you into a good school here. She said she hates England.

Beat.

Kulwant No, she couldn't mean that. I've got to go back to school.

Titoo She's gonna put you in a school here. You're gonna be an Indian boy like me!

Titoo *laughs.* **Kulwant** *goes and sits against a wall at the edge of the roof.*

You wanna fly the kite again?

Kulwant It's stupid having string with glass on it.

Titoo What good would it be without the glass?

Short pause.

Kulwant I hate this place. Everything's so dirty. Why don't people keep it clean?

Titoo You're right. Indians are filthy people. The whole of India should be given a bath! You write a letter to Mrs Ghandi in English. Tell her how they do things in England.

Kulwant You can't even get proper chocolate here. Mum got me some yesterday and it tasted like rubber bands.

The girl – **Nita** *– gets up and goes over to* **Kulwant***.*

Nita I had a bath this morning. I have one every morning.

Kulwant So what?

Beat.

Nita I'm not dirty.

Kulwant I don't mean *you*, I mean the place. There's shit and dust everywhere, and cows just wandering around, and beggars without any arms or legs who should be in a hospital.

Beat.

I've seen where you live as well.

Nita What's wrong with our house?

Kulwant It's not a *house*, it's a room – and there's about six of you living there.

Titoo Her family rent it from your mummy, why don't you tell her to give them some more rooms? You got a big house here, there's plenty of space, lots of empty rooms.

Beat.

Kulwant All right, I'll ask her.

Nita Will you?

Kulwant I might.

Nita I wish we had a big house, so that I could have my own room with my own bed to sleep in. My dad snores all night, especially when he comes in drunk.

Beat.

I'd like a house next to the sea. Have you ever been to the sea?

Kulwant Lots of times.

Nita Really?

Beat.

I've never seen the sea.

Kulwant Why would you want to live there then?

Nita I saw pictures in a magazine.

Titoo Look!

Kulwant *and* **Nita** *look up at the sky.* **Titoo** *looks around at the rooftops and spots somebody – he waves.*

That's Mintoo's kite. Now you'll see.

He starts letting out the string at speed. **Kulwant** *walks over and stands next to him looking up at the kite.*

Kulwant Pull it up, it's sinking too low!

Titoo You can't pull it up, that way you get cut –

Kulwant Let me have a go!

Titoo No – I can't stop!

Suddenly a cry of 'Cutee!' rings out from the other rooftop, **Titoo***'s string goes limp in his hands and falls to the floor. He starts to reel it in.*

Kulwant You got cut.

Titoo Yes.

Kulwant It was so quick.

Titoo Sometimes it is. That bugger Mintoo, he goes and gets his string from Amritsar – best string in the whole Punjab.

Kulwant Why don't we go there and get some?

Titoo It's fifty kilometres from here.

Short pause.

You got some money? We'll go and get another kite.

Kulwant Only if I can fly it.

Titoo I'll teach you.

Scene Two

A Holy Man On The Street.

Kulwant, **Titoo**, **Nita** *and her* **Brother** *walk along the narrow streets,* **Kulwant** *is clutching a new kite.*

A beggar sits resting by the side of the street. He is dressed in the style of a holy man, and has a sword through his mouth. **Kulwant** *stops short and stares at the* **Holy Man** *– the man turns and looks at him.*

Titoo Come on.

Kulwant He's got a big sword through his mouth.

Titoo Yes. Come on.

Beat.

Kulwant Why?

Titoo Ask him.

Kulwant *approaches the man cautiously. He stands near to him for a moment.*

Kulwant Excuse me. Why have you got that sword through your mouth? Doesn't it hurt?

The **Holy Man** *mumbles an incomprehensible reply.*

(*To* **Titoo**.) He can't speak either.

Titoo That's not surprising.

Kulwant Shall we take him to the hospital?

Titoo Why?

Kulwant A doctor could take out the sword. He's not bleeding.

Titoo He doesn't want the sword taken out. He's a holy man.

Kulwant (*to the* **Holy Man**) Shall we take you to the hospital?

*The **Holy Man** shakes his head vigorously.*

Are you a holy man?

*The **Holy Man** nods his head.*

Do you talk to God?

*The **Holy Man** nods again.*

What do you say?

*The **Holy Man** looks baffled. He shrugs.*

Titoo   You never seen one of these types before?

Kulwant   No. I've seen lots of people without arms or legs.

Nita   You shouldn't talk to him anymore.

Kulwant   Why not?

Nita   He might get angry and put the evil eye on us.

Titoo   You talk like your mother.

Nita   Things like that are true.

Kulwant *is looking at the* **Holy Man** *again.*

Kulwant   Shall I give him some money?

Titoo   What you scared of?

Nita   Yes, give him some – he won't get angry then.

Titoo   People like you should go back to the villages where you belong. He can't do nothing to us.

Nita   How do you know.

Titoo   I'm not scared of him! Are you Kulwant – are you scared?

Kulwant   Um, no . . .

Titoo   That's 'cause we're not bumpkins like Nita. You know what I'm gonna do? – I'm gonna go and live in England so I can get away from all the bumpkins in this town.

Nita   (*pulling at **Kulwant**'s shirt*) Let's go and fly the kite – come on.

Titoo   You still think I'm scared.

Nita   I don't want to talk to someone with the evil eye on them.

Titoo   What evil eye?

*He turns on the **Holy Man**.*

You gonna put the evil eye on me, you old codger?

*The **Holy Man** makes no response.*

Are you?

The **Holy Man** *just stares at* **Titoo**. *Suddenly furious,* **Titoo** *grabs the sword at both ends and shakes the* **Holy Man***'s head from side to side, finally pushing him back on the ground and standing over him.* **Nita** *has started to cry – she is holding on to both* **Kulwant** *and her* **Brother**. *The* **Holy Man** *holds his hands out in front of his face, he is moaning gently.*

Pause.

Kulwant   Shall we take out the sword?

Nita   No!

Titoo   Yeah – you take out the sword.

Kulwant *steps forward. He kneels down by the* **Holy Man***'s side.*

Kulwant   Will it hurt you if I take it out?

The **Holy Man** *stares at him in fear.*

I'll do it gently.

He holds the scabbard.

Tell me if it hurts.

He starts to pull on the sword. **Titoo** *looks disinterested and goes and sits a few feet away. Despite their fear,* **Nita** *and her* **Brother** *move in closer to watch.* **Kulwant** *turns around holding up the sword. The* **Holy Man** *continues moaning softly behind them.* **Kulwant** *looks at* **Titoo** *triumphantly.*

Titoo   You going to keep it?

Kulwant *nods.*

Why don't you get rid of that hat? Tell your mother the wind blew it away.

Kulwant *takes off the hat.*

Nita   Can I have it?

Kulwant   She'll see you wearing it.

Beat.

It doesn't matter. Tell her you found it somewhere.

He puts it on her head.

Nita   Is it a hat from England?

Kulwant   Yes.

Beat.

We bought it from a place next to the sea.

Nita   Is it a sea hat?

Kulwant   Yes.

Nita   (*to her* **Brother**) It's a real English sea hat!

Kulwant *goes and sits next to* **Titoo**.

Kulwant   Why are all the houses around here red?

Titoo   It's the old Moslem district. This is where they all used to live.

Kulwant   (*looking around*) They've got lovely patterns on the walls. Where did they go?

Titoo   Who?

Kulwant   The Moslems.

Titoo   A lot of them got killed here. They had their heads chopped off. Their blood covered these streets all over. My granddad used to tell us about it. A few got away and went to Pakistan.

Beat.

Kulwant   Who killed them?

Titoo   People did.

Kulwant   Why?

Titoo   'Cause they were Moslems. It was when the British cut up the Punjab so the Moslems could have their own country.

Beat.

Kulwant   There might be ghosts here at night.

Short pause.

Titoo   Yeah, you never know. Come on, there's a good breeze going now – let's get that kite up.

They get up and walk off, leaving the **Holy Man** *still lying moaning by the side of the street.*

Scene Three

In The Shade With Some Old Women.

Kulwant *sits in the veranda of the house with his* **Mother**, *three* **Old Women**, *and a* **Very Old Man**. *They are sitting on 'manjas': beds made from wood and rope. In one corner of the veranda is a hand operated water pump from which people occasionally come and draw water. All of them are fanning themselves.*

Old Woman 1   He's such a pretty thing.

Old Woman 2   Such a fair skin!

Old Woman 3   Keep him out of the sun, Lakhbir, or he'll go black like us!

Old Woman 2   No, their family have always been fair.

Old Woman 3   Yes, but they looked after their skins – always stayed in the shade. A few days under this sun will turn anybody's skin to leather.

Mother   I had to stop him going up to fly another kite with Titoo – they've been up there all day. Where's the hat I gave you?

Kulwant   It blew away.

Old Woman 1   What's he say?

Mother   Speak in Punjabi to your Aunties, Kulwant.

Kulwant   I'm getting tired speaking in Punjabi all the time, Mum.

Old Woman 1   What's he say?

Old Woman 3   It doesn't sound like a language when he talks. Does he know Punjabi, Lakhbir?

Mother   Yes, he speaks it very well. Speak to your Aunties, Kulwant.

Kulwant *just looks at his feet glumly.*

Old Woman 1   I've heard him speak. He speaks beautifully.

Old Woman 2   He's shy.

Kulwant   No I'm not, I'm bored.

Old Woman 1   What's he –

Mother   Yes, he's shy. He thinks you'll laugh at him.

Old Woman 3   He sounds like a little bird – peek peek peek peek . . .

Kulwant   Why's she saying that? I don't sound like that.

Mother   She doesn't understand you, English sounds strange to her.

Kulwant   Well, she must be stupid then.

Mother   You can't behave here like you do in England. You have to show respect to old people here.

Old Woman 1   How long are you planning to stay this time, Lakhbir?

Mother *looks at* **Kulwant**, *who suddenly shows an interest in the conversation.*

Mother   Well . . .

Old Woman 3   These English, they don't like to stay in India too long – it's too hot and dirty for them.

Old Woman 2   I visited my son in England. They wanted me to stay – but I told them I would die in all that rain and cold.

Old Woman 1   We're used to it here. But children from there, it's difficult for them to adjust.

Mother   Kulwant has no problem with the weather here. He'd stand on the roof all day flying kites if I would let him.

Kulwant   There's nothing else to do.

Mother   That's true.

Old Woman 1   What is?

Mother   He says there's nothing else for him to do here.

Old Woman 2   Children get bored very quickly.

Old Woman 3   We never had the time to get bored. Soon as I could stand up and walk, my family had me helping in the house and out in the fields.

Mother   I will have to find a good school for him.

Old Woman 1   A school?

Mother   Of course. I don't want him to fall behind with his education.

Kulwant   I don't want to go to school here. I go to Dormers Wells.

Mother   There are very good schools in India, better than the ones in England.

Old Woman 3   He'll adjust.

Kulwant   But I *already* go to Dormers Wells.

Mother   Well I can't put you on an aeroplane every day to go to school, can I Kulwant?

Pause.

Kulwant   When are we going back home?

Mother   Don't you like it here?

Pause.

Kulwant   I like flying kites and playing. It's better than going to school.

Mother   This is your *real* home you know.

Kulwant   No it isn't. I'm from London.

Mother   But this is where you're really from.

Old Woman 3   Tell the boy to speak Punjabi.

Old Woman 1   He's probably scared of you.

Old Woman 3   Why?

Old Woman 1   Have you looked in the mirror recently?

Old Woman 3   That's true. He probably thinks I want to eat him up. Eh, is that what you think, boy?

Kulwant *shakes his head.*

He does understand!

Old Woman 1   Of course he does.

Old Woman 3   Are you scared of us old women, Kulwant?

Kulwant   No.

Old Woman 3   Then come here and sit with us. I can hardly see you with these eyes of mine.

A pause. **Kulwant** *gets up hesitantly and walks slowly to the bed where the* **Old Women** *are sitting. He stands in front of them.*

Old Woman 2   You know, all the girls will break their hearts on the ground for you in a few years.

Kulwant   Why?

Old Woman 1   His wedding will be a thing to see, I hope I live long enough.

Old Woman 3   In the old days we could have found him a wife right now!

Old Woman 1   He should meet my granddaughter. She's pretty as a picture. What do you say, Lakhbir?

Old Woman 2   You're thinking ahead aren't you?

Old Woman 1   No harm in that.

Kulwant   I'm never going to marry anybody anyway.

Old Woman 3   Look how these children talk nowadays!

Old Woman 1   Yes, they're born with their own minds now.

Short pause.

The children were telling me you were flying kites all day on the roof.

Kulwant   Yes.

Beat.

Then we went to get another one and we went to where the Moslems all got killed.

Beat.

Old Woman 2   In the old town?

Kulwant   Yes. They had beautiful houses there. Who killed them all?

Short pause.

Old Woman 3   Boy's got a curious mind – maybe he'll be a policeman, eh?

Kulwant   Did they catch the people who killed them all?

Old Woman 2   No. Nobody was caught.

Kulwant   Who killed them?

Old Woman 2   People did.

Kulwant   What people?

Old Woman 1   People from this town. Lots of people were killed then – Moslems and Sikhs and Hindus.

Kulwant   Oh.

Beat.

There must be lots of ghosts then.

Beat.

Old Woman 1   Yes, there are I suppose.

Beat. She opens a small purse and takes out some change.

Go and buy yourself some ice-cream from the stall.

Kulwant   Thanks, aunty.

He runs off.

Scene Four

At The Stall Eating Tutti-Frutti.

A small open-fronted stall which sells cigarettes, soft drinks, tea, snacks and ice-cream. A variety of people are standing around drinking tea, eating and chatting. **Titoo** *stands smoking a cigarette and joking with the* **Stallholder**. *The* **Holy Man** *sits to one side watching the comings and goings.*

Kulwant *enters, he is carrying the sword he took from the* **Holy Man**.

Titoo   Hey Kulwant! You still got the sword – I thought your mother would have taken it. (*To the* **Stallholder**.) Have you met the boy from London?

Stallholder   London, eh? (*Smiling.*) Which part of India is that in?

Titoo   You see these village types Kulwant, they still think the earth is flat!

Stallholder   What shape do *you* think it is then Professor?

Kulwant   Have you got any ice-cream?

Stallholder   The best ice-cream in all India, sahib!

Kulwant   Have you got vanilla?

Stallholder   Vanilla!

Titoo   He only has one flavour – tutti-frutti.

Kulwant   Is that all?

Beat.

I'll have that then.

Stallholder   (*putting the ice-cream into a cone and handing it to* **Kulwant**) Best tutti-frutti you'll ever taste!

Kulwant *makes to hand him some money.*

Free to you, sahib!

Titoo   What did your mum think of the sword?

Kulwant   Nothing. I hid it.

Titoo   You going to use it? You going to chop off some bugger's head with it?

Kulwant   I might do.

Stallholder   How's the tutti-frutti, sahib? Tasty tasty, eh?

Kulwant   It's nice.

Stallholder   Nicey nicey, eh?

Titoo   Anyone give you trouble, just swipe off his head with one stroke. Then pick up the head, look the bloke in the eye and tell him, 'That'll teach you to mess with a boy from London.'

Kulwant   He'd be dead by then.

Titoo   No he wouldn't, I've seen it for myself.

Kulwant   What?

Titoo   We had a bloke here in the market – just up over there. Fell off his bicycle and got his head cut clean off by the wheel of a truck – (*To the* **Stallholder**.) you remember that, Ramchand?

Stallholder   Last July it was.

Titoo   Some joker went and picked up the head. There was a big crowd there in seconds. We all saw the face. I swear to you that head was blinking, his eyes were moving around looking at us all – he looked surprised, kind of.

Stallholder   His lips moved –

Titoo   – That's right! His lips moved too. Must have been like that for a couple of minutes, his head looking around at all of us, and us just staring back. Some bloke even went over and had a word with it.

Kulwant   What did he say?

Titoo   He said, 'Bad luck, old boy.' He reckons the head raised its eyebrows, kind of like a shrug saying, 'Well, that's life.' The Police came and carried the head off to the bloke's house for the wife to identify.

Beat.

Kulwant   (*touching the blade*) I don't think this is sharp enough to cut off anyone's head.

Titoo   That's easy to fix.

Beat. **Kulwant** *notices the* **Holy Man** *staring longingly at his sword. He walks over to him.*

Kulwant   Would you like an ice-cream?

Silence.

It's nice, I'll buy you one if you like.

The **Holy Man** *looks sadly down at the ground.*

(*To* **Titoo**.) He doesn't talk.

Titoo   Some of these holy types are like that. They take all sorts of secret vows.

Kulwant   (*to the* **Stallholder**) Could I have another one, please? I'll pay this time.

The **Stallholder** *makes another cone.*

Stallholder   No need for money, sahib, this one is for God.

He hands the cone to **Kulwant** *who takes it and offers it to the* **Holy Man**.

Kulwant   It's tutti-frutti.

The **Holy Man** *hesitates for a moment, then reaches out and takes the cone.* **Kulwant** *watches him as he eats.*

Do you like it?

The **Holy Man** *nods.*

Stallholder   You will certainly have a long and happy life.

Kulwant   Why?

Stallholder   Because you have made an offering to a man of God.

Titoo   If he's a 'man of God', I must be the President of India!

Kulwant   Maybe he really is.

Beat.

Would you like your sword back?

The **Holy Man** *looks at the sword.*

Would you like it back?

Beat.

We shouldn't have taken it from you.

He offers the sword.

You can put it back through your mouth if you like.

The **Holy Man** *reaches out and takes the sword.*

Beat.

Holy Man   Thank you.

Titoo   Oi, I thought you weren't allowed to speak!

Holy Man   Why?

Titoo   Don't you types have a vow of silence or something? He gives you an ice-cream and you forget all about religion. Next thing you'll be asking me for a fag.

Holy Man   I took no vow of silence.

Titoo   So how come I never heard you talk? You been coming round this way for years.

Holy Man   I always had the sword in my mouth.

Stallholder   Didn't it ever rust, the sword – with all your spit on it, I mean?

Holy Man   I take it out every night and clean it.

Long beat.

No one ever talked to me.

Titoo   That's 'cause they thought you couldn't.

Kulwant   Would you like another ice-cream?

Stallholder   He'll get fat!

Titoo   You want a cigarette?

The **Holy Man** *nods –* **Titoo** *gives him a cigarette and a light.*

Strange kind of holy man you are.

Holy Man   I smoke sometimes. I think I do enough for God.

Kulwant   Are you going to put the sword back in?

Holy Man   I feel strange walking around without it.

Kulwant   Is it some kind of special sword?

Beat. The **Holy Man** *looks at him for a moment, as if sizing him up.*

Holy Man   It is to me. It means something very special.

Kulwant   What?

Holy Man   It means that I have decided to live my life in one way, for one thing only. Without the sword, I would lose my way. My soul would be lost.

Kulwant   Why don't you do a job instead?

Holy Man   This is my job – I was appointed to it by God. He came to me in a dream and told me that this was what I was to do.

Stallholder   I hope you got yourself a better pension scheme than me!

Holy Man   (*ignoring him*) When people see me, they are perhaps reminded of their souls. They remember their connection to the divine.

Kulwant   Oh.

Stallholder   You know something, I think he's right! I'll give all my money to charity and go to work on a leper colony.

Titoo   Yer arms would drop off. Maybe your dick too.

Stallholder   It would be worth it for my ticket to heaven. Perhaps then in my next life I would be born a rich man!

Titoo   I wouldn't want my dick dropping off, not for anything. I run a mile if I see a leper.

Kulwant   (*to the* **Stallholder**) You're going to have another life?

Stallholder   Of course. That's why I have to watch it, I don't want to come back as a donkey or something. I want to come back as a boy from London!

Titoo   That's what Hindus reckon, see – that we keep coming back as something over and over. If you live good, then you come back as something better than you were last time round.

Kulwant   Do you believe that?

Titoo   Suppose I do.

Kulwant   I don't, I think it's silly.

Titoo   That's 'cause you're a Sikh, not a Hindu. Why don't you wear a turban?

Kulwant   I don't know.

Titoo   Would you want to?

Kulwant   Everybody at school would make fun if I did.

Beat.

I don't think they look nice. They make you look too different.

Short pause.

I think my mum wants me to go to school here.

Titoo   Told you. What you gonna do?

Kulwant   I'm gonna write my dad a letter and tell him to come and take me home.

Titoo   Why don't you tell your mum to?

Kulwant   She always says yes to everything, then she never does what she promised.

Titoo   You think he'll come and get you?

Kulwant   I'll tell him in the letter I hate it here.

Titoo   Do you?

Kulwant   No, but I will if I have to go to school here. I don't want to live here forever.

Titoo   You might get used to it.

Kulwant   No, I won't.

Titoo   How d'you know?

Kulwant   (*getting angry*) I just do, that's all!

Pause.

Titoo   What's it like there then, where you come from?

Kulwant   In London?

Titoo   Yeah. Has everybody got lots of money like you?

Kulwant   I haven't got lots of money.

Titoo   Compared to us, you have.

Stallholder   Oh yes! Compared to us, you are a little Maharaja!

Kulwant   Do you think so?

Short pause.

We've only got a small house in England. It's not like the one here. But I prefer our house there. This one's so old and dirty. We've got a television as well.

Titoo   What, your own one?

Kulwant   Everybody has.

Titoo   You hear that, Ramchand?

Stallholder   Doesn't surprise me – that's why they ruled over us and not the other way around, eh?

Titoo   How long would it take you to save enough money to buy a television?

Stallholder   (*pretending to make a calculation on his fingers*) Well, if I worked overtime, about four or five lifetimes.

Pause.

Titoo   I'd like to go there. I'd like to go and live there and be like them.

Beat.

You reckon I ever could?

Kulwant   I suppose so. You just go on the aeroplane from Delhi.

Titoo   I've never even been to Delhi. You've seen more of India than me and you've only been here a few days.

Kulwant   I saw the pyramids in Egypt from the aeroplane. We landed in Cairo and I saw them. I want to go there properly when I grow up and go and explore inside them. They've got treasure in some of them that nobody's ever found.

Short pause.

Titoo   I could come with you, couldn't I, if I came and lived in England? We could go and find that treasure together.

Kulwant   You could come if you want.

Titoo   Are you really going to do it?

Kulwant   Yes, I am.

Beat.

Titoo   Can you see into the future, Holy Man?

Holy Man   Sometimes.

Titoo   You reckon we'd find that treasure?

Holy Man   No. But it is always good to look for precious things.

Titoo   What d'you know? We might find it. I tell you what, if we did, maybe I'd come back and build you a little temple.

Holy Man   Thank you.

Titoo   You got any pictures of those pyramids?

Kulwant   I've got a whole book about them.

Titoo   I just wanna see the pictures, so I can figure out a plan.

Stallholder   You wouldn't be able to *read* the book anyway, Mr Big Explorer.

Titoo   Yeah, but I'm good with my hands. Kulwant could take care of the reading side.

Short pause.

We're gonna do it you know, you an' me. We'll find the gold in those pyramids.

Kulwant   Some of them have curses though.

Titoo   Curses?

Kulwant   Yes. There was a king called Tutankhamun. The people that found him all died because of the curse.

Titoo   Really? They all died from the curse? Shit.

Beat.

You can do something about curses, can't you, Holy Man?

Holy Man   Well . . .

Titoo   Come on – what's the use of believing in God so much if you can't even do something about some old curse?

Beat.

Look, we'll cut you in on anything we find. That's a promise.

Short pause. The **Holy Man** *gestures for* **Titoo** *and* **Kulwant** *to approach him and kneel. They do this – he waves his hands over them and chants a brief prayer.*

Titoo   Is that it? Are we done?

Holy Man   Yes.

Titoo   Great!

They stand up.

(*To* **Kulwant**.) We'll be okay now, Hindu magic's the most powerful of them all.

Kulwant   Are you sure?

Titoo   Course I am – we've got a whole bunch of really strong gods behind us.

Kulwant *looks up at the sky.*

Kulwant   It's getting dark. Look at those clouds.

Stallholder   The monsoon rains will be here soon.

Titoo   You ever seen a monsoon?

Kulwant   No.

Titoo   It rains all the time.

Nita *approaches with her little* **Brother.**

Nita   Your mummy's calling you.

Kulwant   What does she want.

Nita   She wants you to come home.

Kulwant   Tell her you couldn't find me.

Nita   That would be telling a lie!

Beat.

She made me give the hat back.

Kulwant   You shouldn't've let her see it!

Beat.

Now she'll make me wear it again.

Nita   Are you coming?

Short pause.

Kulwant   (*to* **Titoo**) What are you going to do?

Titoo   I'm gonna go out with my friends and have fun with them.

Kulwant   Don't you have to go home as well?

Titoo   Na. I can go home anytime I like. Sometimes I stay out all night if I want.

Beat.

Nita   Your mum said if you wouldn't come with me, she'd have to come and get you herself.

Kulwant   (*to* **Titoo**) You're lucky you are.

Beat.

I'd better go.

Titoo   We'll fly that kite tomorow.

Kulwant   Will you come in the morning?

Titoo   Depends what I'm doing.

Kulwant *walks off followed by* **Nita** *and her* **Brother**.

Act Two

Scene One

In The Alley Playing Cards.

A year after the events of the first act. **Kulwant** *and* **Titoo** *sit playing cards in an alley with several other boys. The* **Holy Man** *sits to one side watching them.*

Kulwant   (*laying down his cards*) Yes!

Boy 1   How's he do it?

Boy 2   He cheats!

Kulwant   You shut your mouth.

Titoo   He had a good teacher.

Kulwant   You lot are just useless.

Boy 3   Listen to the big-shot London boy, eh? You think you're special.

Titoo   He is.

Boy 3   Yeah? He doesn't even go to school or nothing.

Kulwant   That's because I don't like the schools here. They're all rubbish. The teachers don't even know how to speak English properly.

Boy 4   I wish I didn't have to go to school.

Kulwant   Just tell your mum, like I did. She just takes me out when I tell her I hate it and tries to get me into another one.

Boy 4   That's your mum. My mum just hits me when I say I feel like staying home sometimes.

Kulwant   Why don't you be sick then?

Boy 4   Then she just makes me drink cod-liver oil before hitting me and sending me to school.

Kulwant   You lot want another game then?

Boy 1   No way, you got all my money. I'm off.

He gets up to go.

You coming, you lot?

Boy 3   Yeah, come on.

The boys get up and leave.

Titoo   What you wanna do?

Kulwant   I don't know.

Beat.

I got a letter from my dad.

Titoo   What he say?

Kulwant   Nothing much. He said he might come to India.

Titoo   That's good.

Kulwant   He said that in his last letter. He just writes the same things over and over again. He wrote a letter to my mum this time as well. It's the first one he wrote her since we came.

Titoo   He must still be angry.

Kulwant   Maybe he isn't now.

Short pause. **Titoo** *takes out a packet of cigarettes.*

Titoo   You want a fag?

Kulwant *looks over at the* **Holy Man**. **Titoo** *registers this.*

Kulwant   No thanks.

Titoo   What you scared of him for?

Kulwant   I'm not.

Titoo   Nobody worries about him, but I noticed how you're different when he's around.

Kulwant   I'm not different.

Titoo   You scared of him or something?

Kulwant   I just don't feel like smoking, that's all.

Short pause.

Titoo   (*getting up*) I got to go.

Kulwant   Where to?

Titoo   I got things to do.

He walks off. **Kulwant** *sits shuffling the deck of cards. The* **Holy Man** *takes out a small book and starts to read.* **Kulwant** *watches him for a moment.*

Kulwant   Do you read a lot of books?

Holy Man   No, only this one.

Kulwant   What's it about?

Holy Man   It's about something different every time I read it.

Kulwant How come, do the words change?

Holy Man Yes.

Kulwant Is it a magic book then?

Holy Man No.

Pause.

Kulwant I wouldn't have believed you anyway, if you said it was.

Beat.

Why didn't you ever put the sword back in your mouth?

Holy Man Because you took it out.

Kulwant So what? I gave it back to you, didn't I?

Holy Man Perhaps you were sent to take it out.

Kulwant Sent by who?

Holy Man Sent like the dream that told me to put it in.

Short pause.

Kulwant Nobody tells the truth about anything do they?

The **Holy Man** *looks at him.*

You can't listen to anybody.

He gets up and walks off.

Scene Two

Flying A Kite Without Titoo.

Kulwant *stands on the rooftop flying a kite.* **Nita** *sits watching him, she is sewing a pattern into a piece of cloth.*

Nita Why don't you fly kites with Titoo anymore?

Kulwant I can fly them better without him.

Nita But he taught you.

Kulwant He says he doesn't like flying them now. He always wants to do boring things.

Nita What boring things?

Kulwant He just wants to stand around talking to his friends all the time.

Nita Oh.

Beat.

What do they talk about?

Kulwant   I don't know. Girls and things.

Beat.

They're always asking me what English girls are like.

Nita   Oh.

Long beat.

What *are* they like?

Kulwant   How should I know?

Nita   Are they pretty?

Kulwant   I don't know, do I?

Nita   You must do, you must have seen lots of them.

Beat.

They have golden hair, don't they?

Kulwant   *Who* do?

Nita   English girls.

Kulwant   Some of them, I suppose.

Nita   I wish I had golden hair.

Kulwant   You'd look stupid.

Nita   Why?

Kulwant   Because you're so brown. You'd look like a freak.

Pause. **Nita** *looks hurt.*

Nita   You think I'm ugly!

Kulwant *looks around at her.*

Kulwant   No I don't.

Short pause.

Nita   Do you think I'm pretty then?

Kulwant   What does it matter what I think? I don't know about things like
that.

Nita   Things like what?

Kulwant   Yunno, *girls things*.

Nita You do think I'm ugly, don't you? You just don't want to say it. (*Standing up.*) Go on, just say it! I don't care!

Kulwant You're not ugly!

Nita Am I pretty then?

Short pause.

Kulwant (*mumbling*) Suppose so.

Nita What?

Kulwant Yeah, you're pretty.

Pause.

Nita Do you want to kiss me then?

Kulwant No!

Nita Why not, if I'm pretty?

Kulwant Just 'cause you're pretty or whatever, doesn't mean I have to kiss you like we're married or something, does it?

Beat.

Nita You're just scared!

Kulwant You might have some sort of disease. My whole face could drop off.

Nita I haven't got a disease!

Kulwant How do I know that?

Nita I've been to the doctor!

Kulwant Well you must have had a disease to go to the doctor.

Nita No, I didn't!

Kulwant Why'd you go then?

Nita I just did. My Mum took me.

She walks up to him.

You are scared.

He studiously ignores her proximity.

You are, aren't you?

Beat.

I'm not.

She leans forward and kisses him, they look at each other for a moment, then she runs off giggling. **Kulwant** *is left looking rather shocked. He slowly starts to pull in the kite.*

Scene Three

A Conversation With Mum.

Kulwant *lies in bed reading an 'Archie' comic. His mother enters. He carries on reading.*

Mother   Kulwant.

Kulwant   Mmm?

Short pause.

Mother   What are you reading?

Kulwant   A comic.

Mother   Oh. Is it one of your American comics?

Kulwant   Yeah.

Mother   'Yes', not 'Yeah'.

Kulwant   Mmm.

Pause.

Mother   Are you happy here, Kulwant?

Kulwant   Where?

Mother   Here, in India.

Kulwant   It's okay.

Beat.

Mother   Daddy wrote me another letter.

Kulwant   That's nice.

Mother   Yes it was a nice letter. I'm glad he hasn't forgotten me.

Kulwant   How could he forget you Mum, you've known each other since before I was born.

Mother   But I'm glad he doesn't hate me.

Kulwant *turns the page of his comic.*

Perhaps you should be in a school that you like. With your friends.

Short pause.

Do you still miss your friends?

Kulwant   I see my friends every day.

Beat.

Mother   No, I mean your London friends.

Kulwant   Sometimes.

Mother   You used to miss them a lot, before.

Kulwant *turns the page of the comic again.*

I'm sure they miss you.

Kulwant   I think I like it here better than England.

Mother   Better than England?

Kulwant   Yes.

Mother   Why?

Kulwant   There's more to do here.

Beat.

I'm special here. I've got grown-up friends like Titoo.

Short pause.

Mother   Daddy says he misses you so much.

Kulwant   He should come and see me then, like he promised.

Mother   He wants to, he really does want to see us both, but he can't get time away from work.

Pause.

Titoo's in the hospital.

Kulwant   What's he doing there?

Pause.

Mother   I don't know very much. Somebody just came and told me about it.

Kulwant   Is he sick or something?

Short pause.

Mother   He had an accident.

Kulwant   Really?

Mother   You see, you never listen to me when I tell you not to go round running on the street – it's so easy for boys to get hit by trucks or cars.

Kulwant   Was he hit by a truck?

Mother   I don't know, I think so.

Beat.

They say it was a truck.

Kulwant   Can we go and see him.

Mother   No . . . I don't know where the hospital is.

Kulwant   We can find out, can't we? I want to go and see him.

Pause.

Mother   We can't.

Kulwant   But he's my friend!

Short pause.

Mother   He's not alive any more, Kulwant. He's dead.

Kulwant   Dead?

Mother   You never listen to me when I tell you, do you? You always go playing with him in the worst places. Thank God you weren't with him!

Pause.

Kulwant   Did his head get chopped off?

His **Mother** *looks at him uncomprehendingly.*

Scene Four

Leaving.

Dusk. **Kulwant** *goes to the stall, which is closed. The* **Holy Man** *crouches to one side.* **Kulwant** *walks over and sits down next to him.*

Holy Man   I was watching the sun go down.

Beat.

I like to watch it, and then the moon and the stars. It's never dark.

Short pause.

Kulwant   Why is the stall closed?

Holy Man Ramchand went to the funeral. First time he's closed the stall in years.

Pause.

Kulwant What do you think Titoo will come back as?

The **Holy Man** *looks at him.*

I mean, in his next life. Do you think he's started it yet?

Holy Man Perhaps.

Pause.

Kulwant My mum's taking me back to England. We're going in the morning.

Holy Man Will you come back?

Beat.

Kulwant I don't know. I suppose I'll have to go back to my proper school now.

Pause.

What are you going to do?

Short pause.

Holy Man I would like to go and visit those pyramids you told us about.

Kulwant How will you get there?

Holy Man I'll walk.

Beat.

Kulwant Could you walk that far?

Holy Man I don't know. How far are they?

Kulwant I don't know.

Holy Man Are they as far as Bombay?

Kulwant I suppose they must be.

He gets up. The **Holy Man** *looks at him for a moment.*

Holy Man Never forget, this is where you are from.

Short pause.

Kulwant No, it's not.

He runs off, leaving the **Holy Man** *sitting alone.*

Images Etched on the Memory

Harwant Bains interviewed by Jim Mulligan

The Cowboys of Southall are the group of London-born Asian youths who rampage their way through Harwant Bains's film *Wild West*, which was commissioned by Channel 4 and released in selected cinemas. The characters in the film are based on Harwant Bains's friends who went with him to a comprehensive school in Southall and who played in bands and hung out together. He left that scene to read philosophy at Bristol University and then worked for a few years in an advice centre. At university he had no intention of becoming a writer but at the age of 22 his play *The Fighting Kite* was put on at the Theatre Royal, Stratford East. This was followed by *Blood* and *True Love Stories* at the Royal Court Theatre, and a period as writer-in-residence there.

In his plays, Harwant Bains draws on his experiences without being autobiographical. Two works which deal with aspects of his life are *Two Oranges and a Mango* and *Indian Summer*, both commissioned works, one by BBC2 and the other by the Royal National Theatre. 'My father died in India in 1993 and the BBC asked me if I would be interested in writing about that. At first I didn't think it was a very good idea – the experience was too close to me – but after a while I took the opportunity to turn the experience into a piece of fiction. It's about a man of 30 going to India for his father's funeral and it explores the conflicts for him, and the people around him, caused by the fact that he sees himself as English, whereas they see him as Indian. That is one way of dealing with the contradictions which come out of being somebody who ostensibly is Indian but whose sensibilities come from being English.'

Indian Summer is similarly created from a real experience. At the age of eight, Harwant was taken by his mother for a holiday to India. Three months stretched to six months and six months to two years with no explanation, and then they returned to England. But Kulwant in the play is not Harwant. The incidents are real, but the character is based on a ten-year-old boy in Harwant's family. 'I know this boy very well. He's intelligent, self-sufficient, emotionally tough and inquisitive and I tried to think how he would react in the situation I was once in. I remember at the time, I didn't object. As a child, you don't really question. You accept. In those circumstances, you don't miss the big cultural things but the tiny things, like a bar of chocolate, or some TV programme, or your mates. When I went there, I spoke Punjabi but I often switched into English if I wanted to feel superior or if I didn't want the others to understand what I was saying to my mother.'

The play is set about 20 years ago, when the partition of India and Pakistan was fresh in the minds of the people, and the terrifying riots were not just vivid in their memories but many of them had actually taken part, killing their neighbours because they were of a different religion. Kulwant comes into this society and is part of it, and yet detached from it, for two years.

'I was asked by the National if I would like to write a play for young people and when I said "yes" I was given a free hand. I had just finished *Two Oranges and a Mango* and I thought I would like to delve a little bit more into my past. When I started writing, I didn't have a story, but I had a few images of India. One of them was flying a kite on the roof and the other was The Holy Man. That is something you don't forget. I was walking down the road and I saw this man with a huge sword stuck through his cheeks. I never spoke to him, there was no kind of relationship, but as he walked past me, the image was etched on my memory. *Indian Summer* is unusual in that it only took two weeks to write, and once it was written I hardly changed it. I usually write quickly to deadlines, but not that quickly. With me there is a long gestation period and then, once I have met the characters in my imagination, I can start writing. Normally I write quite a lot of rubbish, then gradually begin to feel it's authentic, that a real voice is speaking. From then on I just flog away at it. With this play, it was almost as if I was plugged into something outside myself. I don't know how it works. In a sense you seem to be taking dictation so that at the end you are not aware of the meanings of what you have written.'

Once a play is written, Harwant Bains is happy for audiences, directors, and actors to interpret and discover meanings but as a writer he knows that when he is writing badly he is forcing the images and symbols. These have to be subconsciously present to be effective. He is suspicious of too much analysis of his work. When he writes, he tells a story as well as he can without working at symbolism or themes, but he concedes that the Holy Man at least is a symbolic presence as well as being a real character. And it is possible, he says, that the theme of decapitation is present in the play without his realising it. The conflict of two cultures is certainly a theme, but *Indian Summer* is about more than that.

'I find questions like: "Are you torn between two cultures?" irrelevant. They presuppose that I have some choice. In a sense I do, in that we all create our cultural vision, but once we have chosen our cultural parameters, we generally stay within them. *Indian Summer* is not constrained by differences in cultures. It is a hopeful play. It is about innocence and emerging from innocence. I hope Kulwant is going to grow into an interesting man and the Holy Man is going to find something more for himself. The play is about the optimism of childhood and the possibility of discovering new paths.'

Harwant Bains's stage plays include *Fighting Kite*, performed at the Theatre Royal, Stratford East in 1987; and *Blood*, performed at the Royal Court Theatre in 1989 (and published by Methuen) which begins with a child witnessing the murder of his parents during Partition in India. His films include the prize-winning *Wild West* (Channel 4), a zany comedy which follows the fortunes of that total contradiction in terms an Asian Country and

Western band; and *Two Oranges and a Mango* (BBC), a fictional account of his own return journey to India to light his father's funeral pyre. He was Writer in Residence at the Royal Court from 1988 to 1989.

Indian Summer

Production Notes

Setting and staging
Indian Summer is set in the Punjab of the 1970s, at a time when it was twice the
size it is now, with Moslems, Sikhs and Hindus all living together. The
settings are extremely simple and include, in Act I, the roof-top of a house
(suitable for kite-flying) in a medium sized Indian city; a narrow street in the
Moslem district – possibly suggesting the red houses with rich patterns on the
walls; the veranda of a house with manjas (beds made from wood and rope),
plus a hand-operated water pump; an open-fronted stall selling, among other
things, tutti-frutti ice cream. In Act II there are just three scenes: an
alleyway, the roof-top, and a bedroom.
NB. All these settings could be created by a mixture of neutral rostra, perhaps
a few vertical 'flats', plus imaginative lighting.

Lighting in general is bright, to reflect the heat and atmosphere of this city
during an Indian summer. It should create contrasts: for example, the
comparative shade of the veranda and alleyway to the glare of heat hitting the
roof-top. The setting is very specific and **music**, if used, could effectively
create the right atmosphere for this environment. Introducing a mixture of
live and recorded music with genuine Indian instruments would be a good
approach.

Projection slides/photography might be used to locate the play. Costumes
might be authentic or stylised, but some attempt ought to be made to
emphasis Kulwant's 'otherness'.

Casting
Though the setting is India, parts need not be cast according to the age,
gender or the culture of the performer. The play is appropriate for a cast
numbering thirteen to fifteen. Kulwant and Nita are in their early teens.
Titoo is of a similar age, but is much more 'streetwise'. There are four other
boys and Nita's younger brother. The adults are Kulwant's mother, the Holy
Man, three old aunties, an old man, and the ice-cream seller. The play is
suitable for a young audience of about ten upwards.

Questions
1. How is Kulwant's Englishness magnified by his arrival in India? What
    does he expect the people and the place to be like?

2. Why has Kulwant come to India?

3. Titoo's experience is limited – he hasn't had access to TV, books, or

travel. What does he expect Kulwant to be like? How does he imagine London?

4. Kulwant gains status when drawing out the Holy Man's sword. Why does he replace it?

5. What is the importance of the kites? What do they symbolise?

6. What is it that allows Kulwant to accept Titoo's death so easily?

7. What new perspective on life do the characters in the play discover during its course?

8. We first meet Kulwant four to five days after his arrival in India. In Act II we see him one year later. How can this passage of time be expressed on stage?

Exercises

1.　i　Establish what the characters do from moment to moment by charting their various journeys through the play.

　　ii　Decide how they affect one another, for example Kulwant behaves differently when the Holy Man is present.

　　iii　Take an extract, e.g. Act II Scene 2, Kulwant's dialogue with Nita. Decide what each character wants from the other.

　　iv　In a group of six, improvise around the situation in, for example, Act I Scene 3, with the three old women, an old man, Kulwant and his mother. Concentrate on how the characters move, and how they are affected by the heat. Contrast the movements of the grown-ups with Kulwant's own way of moving. Now read through the scene. Decide how the speech patterns vary. Compare the rhythm in this scene, which moves at quite a pace, with the opening of Act I.

2. Notice the 'beats' in the scene. Each one represents a thought. Run through the scene, acknowledging the beat, and asking the characters what they are internalizing during the beat. For instance:

Titoo　Can I ask you something?
Kulwant　All right.
Titoo　Why are you wearing that big hat?
Beat.
Kulwant　Mum told me to. She doesn't want me getting burned out in the sun.

Experiment with using live music, or simply abstract sounds created by the group, to accentuate the beat where useful.

3. Kulwant's family home in India is a four- to five-storey house in a city of 50–60,000 people. It was built by his grandfather. Kulwant's mother is the landlady. What other factors make Kulwant appear high status?

Decide how this status difference affects the action of the characters on stage.

4.   We learn that Kulwant has arrived in India without his father, and that his father writes only one letter to his mother. Write what might be contained in that letter, showing what prompts her decision to return to England.

5.   One simple way of creating the 'sword through the mouth' effect is for the sword (a) to be made of light plastic, and (b) to have a fairly thin (very blunt!) blade, which the actor playing the Holy Man actually jams across his mouth, and grips with his *back* teeth. The sword should have an elaborate – apparently heavy – handle. The blade should be thin enough for the actor to be able to close his lips – he never actually speaks in this scene. Now experiment with mime. With appropriately large movements on the part of Kulwant, and correspondingly large reactions from the Holy Man, the action should be effective and alarming.

Suzy Graham-Adriani
Director/Producer for BT National Connections

Almost Grown

Richard Cameron

Now, we're almost grown. Then, we were all so young and innocent. We lost it, somewhere along the way. Nothing was ever the same, nor could it be. Maybe because of things we did back then, things we thought were a laugh . . . but weren't to others . . . maybe it all comes back to you, finds a way of getting you back, 'As you sow . . .' and all that. Gets you back worse than you ever thought it could.

Time
Now; some of the recent months bringing us to now; and times from years back.

Place
Somewhere along a river bank, and also houses, a flat, a back yard, a pub and a hospital.

Characters

Scott Carey   *18, at 16, and in-between.*
Scott Carey   *10.*
Dave Marshall   *18, at 16 and in-between.*
Dave Marshall   *10.*
Tommy Fallon   *18, at 17, and in-between.*
Tommy Fallon   *10.*
Stella   *18.*
Melanie Carey   *Scott's sister, 16.*
Elaine Marshall   *Dave's sister, 12.*
Eddie Fallon   *Tommy's brother, 20.*
Christine   *Eddie's girlfriend, 20*
Roberts   *his voice at 15, himself at 18.*

Scene One

Along the river. Late evening. **Scott** *stands looking out over the water. Still, then voices, close, but unseen.*

Young Scott   I'm gunna have a boat.

Young Tommy   A yacht.

Young Scott   Yea. Call it *Scott of the Antarctic.*

Young Tommy   *Tommy's Tornado.*

Young Dave   Yea. Mine'll be . . . *Dave's* . . .

Young Scott   *Dog turd.*

Young Dave   Yeah, I'm sure. Hey, we could have a race round the world.

Young Scott   Yea. Have a crew of all women.

Young Dave   Yea.

Young Tommy   With no clothes on.

Young Scott   Yea.

Young Dave   No, they've got to wear something.

Young Scott   Why?

Young Dave   So I can tell 'em to take 'em off.

Young Tommy   Yea.

Pause. The scene turns into bright day. We see **Young Scott**, **Young Tommy**, **Young Dave**.

Young Dave   I wonder what it's like?

Young Tommy   What?

Pause.

Young Dave   You know.

Young Scott   What?

Young Dave   Being older.

Young Scott   You can do what you want for a start.

Young Dave   No you can't, then, you have to go to work.

Young Scott   I'm not going to work.

Young Tommy   I'm not.

Young Scott   I'll have other people working for me. Have me own factory.

Young Dave   What are you going to make?

Young Scott   I don't know.

Young Tommy   Light bulbs.

Young Scott   Eh?

Young Tommy   Everybody needs light bulbs.

Young Dave   Blind people don't.

Young Tommy   Knives, then. You can't do without a knife.

Young Dave   I'm off to write books.

Young Scott   What books?

Young Dave   Story-books.

Young Scott   School-books?

Young Dave   Adventure-books.

Young Scott   Porny-books.

Young Tommy   Be one of them photographers.

Young Scott   Eh, yea.

Young Dave   Make films.

Young Tommy   Yea. Be an actor.

Young Scott   Get to do sex scenes.

Makes some vaguely sexual sounds. **Dave** *joins in, making it more lively,* **Tommy** *adds to the noise. They fall about laughing.*

Young Tommy   I could do that. It's easy, acting. Dying and that. Go on, shoot me.

Dave *shoots him. He dies.*

Young Scott   What we doing, then?

Young Dave   Dunno. Where shall we go?

Young Scott   Dunno. Nothing to do round here.

Young Dave   No.

Young Scott   Tommy? (*No response.*) Are you dead?

Young Tommy   Yea.

Young Scott   Do you want burying or burning?

Young Tommy   Burning.

Young Scott   (*to* **Dave**) Come on, we'll get some wood.

Young Dave   Petrol. Whoooof!

Young Tommy   (*sitting up*) Put me on a Viking ship. Set light to it. Send me off into the fjords.

Young Scott   The what?

Young Tommy   Fjords.

Young Scott   What's that, then?

Young Dave   It's a Viking word.

Young Scott   What's it mean, then? Come on, Mr Dictionary Dave. You don't know.

Young Dave   I do know, then.

Young Scott   What?

Young Dave   It's where their God lives.

Young Scott   What? Heaven?

Young Dave   Viking heaven.

Young Scott   I bet.

Young Dave   (*to* **Tommy**) It is, isn't it?

Young Tommy   Do what Indians do. Build this raft on stilts. Set light to it. Vultures come and pick your bones.

Scott   There int an 'eaven anyway.

Young Scott   There int an 'eaven anyway.

Young Dave   What is there, then?

Young Scott   Nothing. That's it.

Young Dave   Do you reckon? I don't.

Young Scott   What, then?

Young Dave   You come back.

Young Scott   What as?

Young Tommy   A worm. 'Cos you get eaten by worms, don't you?

Young Scott   Yea and worms get eaten by birds.

Young Dave   Yea and birds get eaten by people. Chickens and that.

Young Scott   Geese.

Young Tommy   Pheasant, partridge. What the queen eats.

Young Scott   So you could come back as the queen.

Young Tommy   Prince Charles.

Young Dave   You can't do that, he's already here.

Young Tommy   So everybody gets to be a king or queen one day.

Young Scott   King Scott.

Young Dave   King HRH David. There was one once in the bible. Maybe it were me.

Young Tommy   Bow down to me you peasants. Tutankhamun Tom.

Young Scott   Yea, but if I die before you, I'll be king before you.

Young Dave   You won't get past being a worm. You might get squashed under somebody's foot before a bird can eat you. What happens then?

Young Tommy   Flies eat you. Lay maggots on you.

Young Scott   What eats flies?

Pause.

Young Dave   (*singing*) I know an old lady who swallowed a fly . . . Perhaps she'll die.

Young Scott   No. No, it's (*Sings.*) She swallowed a spider to catch the fly.

Young Dave   (*singing*) She swallowed a bird to catch the spider.

All   (*singing*) That wriggled and juggled and tickled inside her.

Young Scott   (*singing*) She swallowed a cat to catch the bird.

Young Tommy   (*singing*) She swallowed a dog to catch the cat.

Young Dave   (*singing*) She swallowed a . . . what?

Young Scott   Cow.

Young Tommy   No.

Young Scott   Yes.

Young Tommy   Cows don't eat dogs.

Young Scott   They do in this.

Young Tommy   No they don't.

Young Dave   Anyway, it killed her. She's dead, of course.

Young Tommy   Horse, that's it.

Young Scott   Yea, but she swallowed the cow first.

Young Tommy   No she didn't.

Young Dave   Our Elaine ate a grasshopper once.

Young Tommy   What for?

Young Scott   That's nothing, our Melanie used to eat nuts and bolts.

Young Tommy   You're a liar.

Young Scott   She did.

Young Dave   Nuts and bolts?

Young Scott   Yea.

Young Dave   You liar.

Young Scott   You ask me Mam. She used to have this pram with, like, wing nuts on the hood. Melanie used to undo 'em and eat 'em. She'd shit 'em out, my Mam'd wash 'em, screw 'em back on, and Melanie'd take 'em off and eat 'em again.

Young Tommy   Eeeaaagh!

Young Scott   They went through her about four times.

Young Tommy   Eeeaaaagh! How did your Mam. . . ?

Young Scott   Empty her nappy into a colander and swill it under the tap.

They pretend puking.

Well you have to make sure it's come out the other end, don't you?

They begin to make a move.

Where we off?

Young Tommy   That old lime-kiln we found.

Young Dave   I'm not.

Young Tommy   Why not?

Young Dave   No, let's go nick some apples.

Young Scott   We did that yesterday.

Young Tommy   It goes down miles.

Young Scott   I know. Bottomless pit.

Young Dave   They used to put witches in it.

Young Scott   Yea, I know.

Young Tommy   They dint.

Young Scott   They did, then. (*To* **Young Dave**.) Dint they? Mad women. Lower 'em down and leave 'em to rot.

Young Dave   I bet there's all bones.

Young Scott   No, cause they put lime in and it dissolved 'em, turned 'em to slush.

Young Tommy   I bet.

Young Scott   They did.

Young Tommy   Yea, I bet.

They move off.

Young Dave   Where we off, then?

They are gone. The scene turns back to night. **Scott** *looks across the river. Fade out.*

In the dark.

Roberts   A circle of blue sky in the black. Three black heads against the clouds. Shouting down. A stick comes down. I close my eyes and crouch as it clatters against the wall, clumps into the soft dark next to me. I look up. They're gone. Nothing. Gone away and left me. Some birds fly over. Gone away with her. What are they going to do to her?

Got her in the grass now. I can see it in my head. Holding her down. Up there on top. On top of the kiln. Got her down, doing things. Her too scared to scream.

Scene Two

Nine months ago. **Scott**'s *bedroom.*

Scott (*in career's officer voice*) Now then, lad, let's see. Who are you?

Dave David Marshall, sir.

Scott Well now, David, have you had a think about your future?

Dave Sir?

Scott What do you want to be, lad? What do you want to do with your life?

Dave I wanna be . . . erm . . .

Scott (*singing and playing guitar blues*)
I wanna be a hoochie coochie man
Play my mojo all night long.
I said I wanna be a hoochie coochie man,
Play my mojo all night long.
Gonna find me a loving woman now,
A woman that will do me no wrong.

Pause.

Dave Yea. (*Pause.*) So I told him what everybody else was telling him. I want to be a mechanical engineer, sir.

Scott (*pretending to write it down*) David Marshall. Apprentice prat.

Dave Only thing that came into my head. I couldn't tell him I wanted to be a poet, could I? Can't get a job as a poet.

Scott You should have waffled him like I did. I don't know what I want to do. I just want to be famous. Fast cars. That's all. I'm not bothered how I get there.

Dave No, I've got to take this job now. I've got to contribute a bit at home, with me Dad gone. Our Elaine still at school, and that. You're alright. Your folks can afford to let you go to college. You even get a load for passing your exams.

Scott Yea. That's for my lessons. Putting in for my test next year. Won't need many. I can drive anyway. Been driving an MG.

Dave I might try to do evening classes. Get my Maths this time. I would have liked to have gone. Anyway, I'd never pass.

Scott No. You're thick.

Dave Get lost.

Scott   All the revision you did.

Dave   Yea, well.

Scott   I didn't do any.

Dave   Yea, we know. You pass everything and what I don't fail, I scrape through by the skin of my teeth.

Scott   You've either got it or you ant.

Dave   Yea, well. I'm out in the *real* world now, as me Mam says.

Scott   Plenty of talent at college.

Dave   I heard all the women at this place where I'm going, they initiate you, like.

Scott   How?

Dave   Get your pants down. Tub of grease round your tackle.

Scott   Get out.

Dave   I'm telling you.

Scott   Who told you that?

Dave   Somebody that used to work there.

Scott   Bloody hell.

Dave   I know.

Pause.

Scott   You're not going to stop there, though, are you?

Dave   No. Till I sell one of my stories. Then I'm off.

Scott   'I was raped by twenty sex-crazed women. Apprentice tells of his rite of passage'

Pause.

I wonder what we'll be doing in ten years' time?

Dave   Won't be in this place for a start.

Scott   True.

Dave   Maybe come back to do a book-signing session in town.

Scott   Yeah. I'll come back and drive up and down the high street in my open top sports car. Saturday afternoon. Blonde next to me. All the old mob out shopping, pushing prams. 'Hey, look, Scott Carey. He's making films now'. Stop at the lights and they all mob me for my autograph.

Dave Who's the blonde?

Scott Some film actress I'm working with.

Dave Not Stella, then?

Scott Do me a favour, Dave.

Dave I thought she were, you know . . .

Scott She is. She's alright. But, you know, you move on, don't you? You meet new people. Will be doing. College and that. Otherwise it just gets stale.

Dave Yea.

Scott I've only kept it going 'cos I fancy her Mam.

Dave Do you?

Scott Yea.

Dave How old is she?

Scott Forty?

Dave Forty? Have you . . . you know . . . anything ever . . .

Scott No.

Dave One of my fantasies, that.

Scott Me too.

Dave Hitch-hiking somewhere and this woman stops, gives me a lift. Takes me all the way.

Scott Yea. I think she fancies me.

Dave Who?

Scott Stella's Mam. I were stacking bails of straw one day for 'em. Stella weren't there. She'd gone with her Dad to take the horse to the vet's. Her Mam come in the barn with a drink for me. Gives it to me, sits next to me.

Dave Jesus. Yea, go on.

Scott I didn't have a shirt on. She couldn't take her eyes off. Had this skirt on. I'm telling you.

Dave What?

Scott I knew what she were thinking.

Dave What?

Scott She were like . . . trembling.

Dave *gives a low moan.*

I knew she felt as scared as I did. I should have made a move.

Dave   You should have. I would have.

Scott   You?

Dave   Yea.

Scott   I'm sure.

Dave   I would.

Scott   Like when I set it up for you with our Melanie?

Dave   That were different. I never thought about her that way.

Scott   Not much.

Dave   I never.

Scott   Slept with her bra for a month.

Dave   Yea, alright, Scott.

Scott *laughs.*

You got it for me.

Scott   I got fed up of you asking me to nick it for you.

Dave   Yea, alright. And then you went and told her.

Scott *laughs.*

She thinks I'm a right perv now.

Scott   You are.

Dave   I've never dared look at her since.

Scott   Remember when you brought it to school?

Dave   Leave off.

Scott   What did you do with it?

Dave   You chucked it down that old lime-kiln. Pretended it were Stella's. Last summer. That day we stuck Roberts down.

Scott   Scared him silly.

Dave   Telling me.

Scott   We give him some aggravation, didn't we? Him being new.

Dave   Everybody did. He deserved it, though, didn't he? Going on about army cadets and stuff. Always bragging.

Scott   Yea. Funny kid, really.

Dave   Yea. I tried to talk to him and that. I give up.

Scott   Yea, I know what you mean.

Dave   Never see him around anywhere outside school, do you?

Scott   No.

Pause.

Dave   Served him right. He asked for it.

Scott   What?

Dave   When we left him. Him bragging about how he could climb down with that rope we found.

Scott   I know.

Dave   He must have been a bit thick, not to twig we'd untie it from the tree once he were down.

Scott   Yea. Mind you, it was a bit cruel, leaving him.

Dave   Only to see where Stella and Tommy had got to. We came back.

Scott   Yea, after a couple of hours.

Dave   Chucking lighted grass down to see if we could see him.

Scott   We thought he were dead.

Dave   Well, he wouldn't speak, would he?

Scott   We thought he'd blacked out or something.

Dave   Tried to climb out and fallen back down.

Scott   Yea.

Dave   Then he starts cursing and swearing.

Scott   Tied it back to the tree and ran off.

Pause.

Funny, that day.

Dave   What?

Scott   The way Tommy left.

Dave   I knew he were leaving.

Scott   Yea, but not saying anything to anybody. He goes off down the river with Stella to the stream to fill the bottle . . . they get some water and then he just goes off . . . that's it . . . leaves her to come back on her own.

Dave   Yea, well, he didn't want to talk about it, did he?

Scott   I know, but never saying 'see you' or anything. Just going like that. (*Pause.*) I wonder what he's up to now?

Dave   In nick probably.

Scott   Probably.

Dave   I've seen his brother Eddie a couple of times. He doesn't know anything.

Fade out.

In the dark.

Roberts   Now they're back, like they've never been gone. I can see fire. They're floating down lumps of lighted grass, sending them down on me. Fire floating down, flakes of black straw, falling, crackling. I can see them against the sky as I back against the wall, sliming my arms again. Wet, damp slime. Close my eyes as the fire falls.

Scene Three

Three weeks ago. A back garden. **Eddie** *and* **Tommy** *in suits.* **Eddie** *passes* **Tommy** *a piece of paper.* **Tommy** *reads it.*

Tommy What's that mean, then?

Eddie It's medical for what caused it.

Tommy Oh, right.

Gives it back. Pause.

Eddie It went alright, didn't it? (*Pause.*) Tommy?

Tommy Eh?

Eddie It went off alright.

Tommy Yea.

Eddie You OK?

Tommy Yea. (*Pause.*) You getting married, then?

Eddie Eh?

Tommy You and . . .

Eddie Christine.

Tommy Yea.

Eddie No.

Tommy She's alright.

Eddie Yea.

Tommy I wonder what Mam would have thought of her?

Eddie (*puzzled*) Dunno. She would have liked her.

Tommy *looks at him.*

Maybe not. (*Pause.*) Never had much of a life, did she?

Tommy No, not much.

Eddie Better off where she is.

Tommy Bin brain dead for years anyway.

Eddie Yea. I don't know, I suppose she cared about us in her own way.

Tommy Never got round to showing it.

Eddie   Just too far gone with everything. Couldn't say anything worthwhile any more. I'm sure she wanted us around.

Tommy   No, she didn't.

Eddie   It was him.

Tommy   Yea, well, I never went back and saw her, so that's that. (*Pause.*) If he cleared off once he found out she was ill, why didn't she send for you? She knew where you were, didn't she?

Eddie   I think by then she didn't know much about anything.

Tommy   What is he? What's in his brain to make her block us out, made her so she didn't have any sons any more? How can a woman be so scared of losing him, scared of him being there, she goes along with it when he kicks me out?

Eddie   Go from one bloke that frightens 'em to death to another, some women. Maybe she thought that was what love was all about. Never knew any other kind, with Dad, with him.

Tommy   Yea. He was mental. When you left it was . . .

Eddie   I had to.

Tommy   I know.

Eddie   Should have took you with me. (*Pause.*) Anyway, you've done alright.

Tommy   Have I?

Eddie   I keep hearing bits and pieces. The legend of Tommy Fallon lives on.

Tommy   Huh. I thought I were given a wide berth last night. Parting of the Red Sea in that pub.

Eddie   Yea. Good feeling, though.

Tommy   You get a reputation you have to keep living up to it.

Eddie   What do you mean?

Tommy   I am what they want me to be. What they always had me marked down for even before I did anything. So I don't disappoint 'em. I act the part they want to see.

Eddie   Tough little shit.

Tommy   Yep.

Eddie   Even this afternoon. Nothing on your face.

Tommy   For her? Why should I cry for her?

Eddie   What did you come back for? (*Pause.*) Good to see you, anyway. Two years nearly.

Tommy   Something like that.

Pause.

Eddie   After you ran away from home I got to know some of what went on. Saw some of your mates.

Tommy   What mates?

Eddie   David Marshall. The lad you stopped with the night you left.

Tommy   What did he say?

Eddie   He told me about Spawnail coming at you with a knife

Tommy   He was mental. Did Dave tell you about the dog?

Eddie   What dog?

Tommy   Spawnail's Alsatian.

Eddie   No. What?

Tommy   What he did to it.

Eddie   What?

Tommy   To prove to me Mam how much he loved her. Another row they'd had. She told him she'd had enough, wanted him out. He'd smacked her a good 'un. So he's pleading with her, saying sorry, saying how much he loves her and needs her, and then he says he'll prove it. His dog, his best friend. . . . It were chained up in the yard. Couldn't get away. Went out wi' a kitchen knife and stuck it in its belly. And me Mam fell for it. Holding on to each other, crying their eyes out, while the dog bled to death.

Pause.

Eddie   I got him for you.

Tommy   What?

Eddie   When I heard how he'd been knocking you about. I got hold of him.

Tommy   What did you do?

Eddie   I collared him one night, coming down the backs. He never knew what hit him.

Tommy   What did?

Eddie   Clumped him with a coal shovel. I hurt him. Broke a few bits. Bloodied his best shirt for him.

Pause.

Tommy   The night I left she told me as far as she was concerned she had no children. I went mad. He come at me. I was smashing everything. I said I'd never go back. Never. She said she never wanted me back. Ever.

I made up me mind I were gunna clear off, well out of it, well away, get as far away as I could. Go places, abroad and that. Travel the world, nick a bit, work a bit, scrounge my way around. But when I got to the end of our street, it started to hurt. Cuts, bruises. I thought he'd smashed me back in, and her. Thumping. It were killing. So I went to Dave Marshall's, stopped there the night. Thought I'd get off on my travels in the morning.

Eddie   So that's what you did?

Tommy   I got delayed a bit.

Eddie   How come?

Tommy   I was all set to go that day, made me mind up. Scott Carey came round. We all went down the river. I were thinking all the time, it's OK, when we're there I'll say 'See you, I'm off', and I'll leave them, follow the river downstream. Down to the coast. Catch a ship, stow away, whatever.

Eddie   So what happened?

Tommy   We met this girl we knew from school. Stella. She was with this new kid. Roberts. We were just messing about but she made it clear she fancied me, so we start a bit. . . . He got the hump, so we stuck him down this hole, this old lime-kiln. The other two guard him and me and her go off. She was all over me.

I told her what I was doing, running away. She wanted me to stay at her place. They had this big place, with all these outhouses. You can stay there, she says. And every night I'll bring you food and we'll do whatever you want. So I did. I went with her. Left Dave and Scott, and Roberts down the hole, and we just went off.

Stayed for about three weeks. Her dad was a doctor. Her Mam had a sports car. MG. They never knew I was there. I used to watch 'em come and go, went in the house when they'd gone. Massive house. Full of antiques. Guns and stuff. Her Mam had this head on her dressing table with a wig on it. Stella used to put it on and that. She got so . . . like she wanted to get caught. Got a real kick out of it. She was weird. So I left. I didn't take anything. I could have done. Easy.

Pause.

Eddie   You won't know about Dave Marshall's sister, will you?

Tommy   Elaine?

Eddie She was hit by a car. She's alright. Well she's not, but she's alive. She's still in a coma. Three months. They never found the driver.

Tommy Jesus.

Eddie Just left her in the road.

Tommy I might go round.

Christine *arrives.*

Eddie Yes. Must have been drunk or nicked the car or something.

Tommy Bastards.

Chris Here you are.

Eddie Yea.

Chris Are you coming?

Eddie In a bit.

Chris I think your Mam's brother and his wife are wanting everyone gone now.

Eddie Yea, right.

Tommy Is there any sandwiches left?

Chris I've put you a plateful on the sideboard.

Tommy Oh, right.

He goes.

Chris We'll make a move, then, eh?

Eddie Yea.

Chris It went off alright, didn't it?

Eddie Yea.

Chris Tommy been alright?

Eddie Yea. He's fine. Wouldn't let it show anyway.

Chris You?

Eddie Yea, I'm alright. Chris?

Chris Mmm?

Eddie I said I'd ask you if he could stay over at the flat. Just tonight.

Chris Course he can. He's your brother. You don't have to ask.

Eddie It's your flat.

Chris It's our flat.

Eddie   I'll tell him, then.

They go. Fade out.

In the dark.

Roberts   And in my head there's me and my Dad at school at the
headmaster's, my Dad in his uniform and the headmaster as shit-scared of
him as all the kids *he* makes scared, while my Dad goes at him with his voice,
makes him look more and more a fool, and I'm loving it because I know he's
got to send for Tommy Fallon, David Marshall and Scott Carey. Yea. All get
lined up outside. Fallon threatening, smirking. What can the headmaster do
anyway? The look says it. My Dad sees it. Fallon knows my Dad'll get him.
One dark night. Each of them. My Dad's got stuff. Knows stuff. He was in
the SAS, wasn't he? He'll get you for this. Leaving me down here. Get you. In
the cinema. Watching. Sat with your mates, your girl. My Dad behind you.
He'll cheesewire you. You won't even know. Too late. Nobody'll know till the
film finishes and they find you. Give you a nudge and your head drops into
your lap. My Dad's gonna kill you for this!

Scene Four

Three months ago. Scott's house. **Scott** *some way off from* **Stella***, who is looking at him.* **Melanie** *watches.* **Stella** *feels her watching, turns to her.*

Stella Melanie.

Melanie What?

Pause. **Melanie** *isn't going anywhere, she wants to hear this.*

Stella (*to* **Scott**) It's alright, you can say it, you know.

Scott *moves further away.*

What have I done?

Scott Nothing.

Stella I don't –

Scott It's not you.

Stella What, then? What?

Scott Stella . . .

Stella What?

Scott I just –

Stella Somebody at college.

Scott No.

Stella What, then? Scott, I just – just let's try. I know you get fed up of me at times. I know you only come round because you've nothing else to do sometimes. I know. We've had some good times, haven't we? You know we have. You get on with my family, don't you? They're alright. I don't see you for days. I ring you and –

Scott Jesus. A friend of mine –

Stella What?

Scott A friend, alright? His sister –

Stella A girl?

Scott Well it would be, wouldn't it, if it's his sister.

Stella What girl? You're seeing someone – ?

Scott She's twelve years old.

Stella   What? What are you saying? (*Pause.*) Please, Scott. Talk to me. Why won't you talk to me?

Scott   Go home, Stella.

Stella   Scott.

Scott   Go home. I can't.

Stella   Scott, don't.

Scott   I don't want to see you any more. Alright? What do I have to do, throw you out?

Pause. She won't move. He goes out. Pause.

Melanie   Do you want a drink?

Fade out.

In the dark.

Elaine   Was I little then? Was it yesterday? Or years ago? Not little, no. Never had Sorrow then. He came when I was twelve. Yes. How old am I now? Still twelve? Is this a dream I'm dreaming that same day night, that Saturday, or is this a memory of me then? Me. Elaine. Am I grown old? Who am I now?

Lights up on **Elaine**. *She continues.*

Saturday. Sunny. The grass is high and buzzing. Sorrow hears me call his name. His ears come up and then his head. I call again and he sees me. Comes across the field corner to corner, waits for me to walk the track. Shudders in the sunlight. Nuzzles in my neck. I love you, Sorrow. His eyes love me back. Black eyes. All day. All the long day down, across the fields and lanes, he takes me down the long lanes. Strong, shuddering, safe. Together in the world, ours, and precious, and now.

And then that noise, that sudden sound that sends you up and scared and skidding across the track. A car. Only a little car. Can't see it over the hedge yet, beyond the bend, but there, coming. Roaring. I can't hold you now. You're out of me now it's here. The wheels, the windscreen, those two faces. His face. Her face. His face behind the wheel. A face seeing my face, seeing each other's fear, and Sorrow knows my fear and his own, goes up and back, and I go.

The lights begin to fade.

I'm falling. Falling into the front of the car and far away I hear the sounds . . . voices . . . doors banging . . . a soothing voice . . . a frightened voice . . . inside . . . inside a . . . moving . . . lights passing . . . corridors . . . crying . . . somebody crying.

This is a dream I don't want. Wake me up. Wake me up from this. Take me back to Saturdays and Sorrow. Please. Please God.

Lights out.

In the dark.

Roberts And the straw snap crackles and pops. Open my eyes. Red bits. Is it my eyes in the dark of this hole, or the burning bits of straw?

Oy! Roberts! Something for you. Catch! There's a stick waving, something on the end. Can't see it now. Where is it? Then on the black rocks and stones and sand, something falls, soft, white. I pick it up. What girls wear underneath on top. And I see her in my head now, trying to make a tree cover her, crying in her shame, her dress hanging up on a branch. Too high.

Scene Five

Scott's house. Three weeks ago.

Dave   Much the same. We tell her stories and that. She smiles sometimes. Sometimes I think she knows what's going on. (*Pause.*) I'll get off, then. See you, Melanie.

Melanie   You've only just got here.

Dave   I'll try some other time. It's just by the time I've finished work, got home, had a bath . . .

Melanie   It's hard work, then?

Dave   It's alright. Can't all be idle students, can we? You still at the . . . where you were?

Melanie   Yea.

Dave   Anyway, tell Scott I've been round. Tell him to come round if he wants. I'm still at the same place. Say hello to your Mam and Dad for me.

Melanie   Come in.

She pulls him in. He sees **Stella**.

Dave   Alright? (*Pause.*) I thought Scott might be . . .

Stella   No.

Dave   What's up?

Melanie   We don't see him much.

Dave   Why? What's up?

Pause.

Melanie   He's dropped out of college.

Dave   What?

Melanie   A few months back.

Dave   Why?

Melanie   We don't know why. Dad got a letter from college. He hardly ever went the first term. Dad tried to sort it out. He went back regular for a couple of weeks, and then that was it. (*Pause.*) I don't know what's going on. I've tried to talk to him. Just sits in his room playing his guitar. (*Pause.*) I wish you'd talk to him, David.

Dave   Sure.

Melanie   Mam and Dad are worried sick about him.

Dave   I bet. (*To* **Stella**.) Are you two still. . . ? Sorry. I'm sorry, Stella, none of my business.

Stella   It's alright. No secret. We finished. He finished.

Melanie   He won't talk to her.

Dave   That's stupid.

Melanie   I know.

Dave   So what's he doing with his days, then?

Melanie   Up town all day, probably. I don't know.

Dave   Packed it all in. The fool. He could have sailed it.

Melanie   Will you talk to him?

Dave   Yea. Course.

Melanie   Thanks.

Dave   I will.

Melanie   You were his best friend.

Dave   Me?

Melanie   You know you were. He always looked up to you.

Dave   Did he?

Melanie   Yes.

Dave   I always thought he thought I was a bit of a jerk.

Melanie   No.

Dave   Always seemed that way, when there was a load of us. (*Pause.*) Funny. I always looked up to him. I did. Everything going for him. You know what I mean?

Melanie   Yes.

Dave   I envied him.

Melanie   Did you?

Dave   You know I did.

Melanie   No.

Dave   I envied him. Is it envy? For having a sister like you.

Melanie   What?

Dave   I know. Stupid. I never thought I'd ever be able to talk to you again after.

Melanie   What?

Dave   You know.

Melanie   What?

Dave   Your thing.

Melanie   My what?

Dave   You know, what Scott got for me.

Melanie   I don't know what you're talking about.

Dave   Really?

Melanie   What? What are you talking about?

Dave   He never told you?

Melanie   Told me what?

Dave   Nothing.

Melanie   What?

Dave   Wait till I see him. I'll kill him. Just forget I said anything, right?

Melanie   I want to know now.

Stella *smiles at him.*

Dave   He told you? Don't, Stella, don't say anything.

Melanie   Tell me.

Dave   I'm off.

Melanie   David.

Dave   See you Mel, see you Stella.

Melanie *takes him out. Comes back.*

Stella   He fancies you.

Melanie   No he doesn't. What was it?

Stella   Yes he does. Do you fancy him?

Melanie   No. What was it?

Stella   You do.

Melanie   I don't.

Fade out.

In the dark.

Roberts   Sick thumping in my chest now, because I know. I know how it will end. Stella won't be able to breathe while they hold her, stop her screaming. She'll try to tell them 'let me breathe and I'll let you do it'. She's fighting for breath but they think she's fighting for her shame, so they keep her mouth covered and she starts to go, slips away into unconscious where it's warm and safe and then on into dead. And when they realize, they roll her over the side of the kiln, down to the track next to the river. I'll hear her body fall outside, feet away, on the other side of the kiln wall, the white dust on her legs, her face, they'll follow her down, scramble down and lift her to the water's edge. Counting as they swing her, then still. Nothing, as she goes up and out. I'll hear her hit the water. A smack and a deep, deep water lunging sound. Platunge. Under, her dust scumming the surface, waiting for her to roll up again slow. Turning in slow motion, carrying her now, down towards the weir.

Scene Six

One week ago. Christine's flat.

Chris Well, how long?

Eddie I don't know.

Chris Have you asked him?

Eddie No.

Chris Well, ask him. Eddie, this is my flat.

Eddie So you keep telling me.

Chris I just want to know. A week, a month, how long?

Eddie Till he's finished what he came for.

Chris What's that? I thought he just came for the funeral.

Eddie So did I. I don't know. I don't know what's going on.

Chris I don't want you getting involved.

Eddie I'm not.

Chris He's not roping us in on one of his jobs.

Eddie I know he's not.

Chris I don't want the police round here.

Eddie Yea, alright, Chris, alright. I heard you. I've got the message. Jesus. What do you take me for? He's my brother. I haven't seen him for two years.

Chris Well, I haven't seen you doing much catching up. He's never here. Out all night.

Eddie So what are you complaining about?

Chris Why is he out all night? What's he doing?

Eddie You ask him, you're so bothered.

Chris I will if you won't.

Eddie Right.

Chris Right. (*Pause.*) Eddie?

Eddie What?

Chris Nothing. (*Pause.*) We don't know anything about his life now.

Eddie   Has he ever given you cause to think him anything other than a good kid?

Chris   No.

Eddie   So leave it at that. What you don't know can't hurt you.

Pause.

Chris   What about you?

Eddie   What about me?

Chris   You're straight with me, aren't you? (*Pause.*) Are there things you haven't told me?

Eddie   I've told you. Who I was, what I was. That was somebody else, Chris. Somebody I walked away from. It's all gone now. I don't want anything else other than what I've got now. This is it. Don't ask me about what was. I want you to . . . your job's to keep me here, now. You know?

Chris   He brings it all back, doesn't he? Something about him. Puts me on edge.

Fade out.

In the dark.

Roberts   And when they've watched the river take her away they come back up to the top of the kiln. My turn now. Can't let me go. Not now. Finish it. Finding rocks, rolling them away from the roots of trees, roll them to the hole in the sky, over and down, one after another, not knowing which one is the one to split my head open. Keep on till I'm crushed and buried.

And my Mam and Dad at my funeral but it's just some of my stuff in a cardboard box because they never found me, just Kelloggs and cassettes in a box, stuff from my room – a colouring-book from infants, a pop-up book, a few photos, a teddy bear from being little called Kelloggs. My Mam crying. A twenty-one-gun salute.

Please God. Somebody. Somebody stop them. Somebody help us.

Scene Seven

Dave's house. Three days ago.

Dave You were kept on the register till Christmas.

Tommy Was I?

Dave We kept saying you'd left, but they wouldn't believe it.

Tommy Too good to be true.

Pause.

Dave How long are you about, then?

Tommy Just till I get a few things sorted.

Dave Yea, I expect there's a bit to do.

Pause.

Tommy I went down the river the other day. Up as far as the lime kiln.

Dave Yea?

Tommy Do you get down?

Dave Not much, not been in ages.

Tommy Still the same.

Dave Yea. Can't mess about much with a river, can they? Messed about everywhere else.

Tommy Yea, a few changes. Different shops and that. I see the Co-op's somebody else now.

Dave It's been about six different shops since you left.

Tommy Has it? I broke in there once.

Dave Did you?

Tommy Years ago. I got in through this skylight. Dropped down into this room. When I put the light on, it was empty, nothing I could use to get back out. I had to break a door down, get these big cardboard boxes, full of Persil or something, drag 'em into the room and stack 'em up so I could climb back out. I never got a thing. (*Pause.*) Mad.

Dave *smiles.*

Tommy What?

Dave Everybody knew you were thieving, we all knew, but you never involved us, it were never mentioned, all that, was it? We never talked about it. Like, being mates was something else.

Tommy Yea. (*Pause.*) You wouldn't believe some of the stuff I nicked.

Dave I don't want to know.

Tommy I never kept a thing. Never sold it, never give it away, just took it, walked through the streets like I was invisible, and dumped it all.

Dave What?

Tommy All of it. Off the bridge into the river. (*Pause.*) It was all so easy. Maybe I was wanting to get caught. I think to start with it was just somewhere to break in to stop the night. Sleep on a shop floor rather than go home.

Dave No wonder you were always falling asleep at school.

Tommy Yes.

Pause.

So you don't reckon you're going to stick it out where you are?

Dave No, not much longer.

Tommy Do you know what you're going to do?

Dave No. I just know I've had enough. There's got to be something else. My own fault, really.

Tommy Why?

Dave Taking books to read in my dinner hour. They always took the piss. I come back from break one afternoon and they'd been in my bag, taken my books out and drilled holes through 'em all.

Tommy Yea, well, bit of a daft thing to do, what do you expect?

Dave Yea, I suppose.

Tommy Chucking darts at that Bible in the youth club.

Dave Yea.

Tommy See who could throw the furthest in.

Dave Yea.

Tommy I won. Got all the way to Deuteronomy.

Pause.

You always had your head in a book.

Dave Yea.

Tommy   Get a job in a library.

Dave   Yea, I wouldn't mind.

Tommy   You never got round to writing your masterpiece, then?

Dave   No.

Tommy   You ought. You were the only one of us I thought would actually finish up doing it, what they wanted to do. (*Pause.*) You ought.

Dave   I might. One day.

Tommy   You ought.

Dave   Yea.

Pause.

Tommy   Our Eddie's doing alright.

Dave   Is he?

Tommy   Got a welding job. Been doing it a bit.

Dave   Yea?

Tommy   Got hisself a girl. Be getting married next.

Dave   Eddie, settling down?

Tommy   I know. She's alright, though. I like her. Christine. It's her flat I'm stopping at. Well, their flat I suppose.

Dave   Oh, right.

Pause.

Tommy   You're not with anybody, then?

Dave   No. Well, sort of. Not really, just seeing somebody.

Tommy   Who?

Dave   Melanie Carey. Scott's sister. Remember?

Tommy   The one you always fancied at school? You finally scored, then?

Dave   I've only taken her out a couple of times.

Tommy   Weren't she . . . Int she a bit young?

Dave   No. Seemed like it then, I suppose. So you lot always used to tell me, anyway. Two years difference then is like, well, it's not like two years now. You know what I mean?

Tommy   Yea. So how's Scott, then? You still see him?

Dave   No.

Tommy   I always thought he'd finish up in a big name band. I wonder if he still plays?

Dave   Dunno.

Tommy   He was good.

Dave   Yea.

Tommy   Well he seemed good to me.

Dave   He was.

Tommy   If you see him, you'll have to say you've seen me.

Dave   I don't see him.

Tommy   When we used to go up the river, camping, lighting fires. Sitting in the dark, him on guitar, you on harmonica, me hitting two sticks together.

Dave   Yea.

Tommy   Some good sessions.

Dave   Yea.

Tommy   Who cares what it sounds like when it's the middle of a wood, middle of the night?

Dave   I've still got the tapes somewhere of us in his shed, when we recorded ourselves that time.

Tommy   Have you?

Dave   Somewhere.

Tommy   We thought we were ace, didn't we?

Dave   We were ace.

Tommy   We were.

Pause.

Well, I'll get off then.

Dave   Oh, right. Good to see you, anyway.

Tommy   Yea, you too. Look after yourself.

Dave   Thanks for coming round.

Tommy   I might go up and see Elaine while I'm here.

Dave   Yea, right.

Tommy   Get that book written, you. I'm waiting to see myself in print.

Dave   Right.

Tommy   I'll get off, then.

Dave I'll come down with you.

They go. Fade out.

In the dark.

Elaine Alone in a dark tower. How long have I been in this place? The window seems so far away. A tiny room but so long to walk across it and see the day outside.

A spot comes up on her.

Lean out on the stone. Feel the warm sun. See the river down there. Winding away. Lost behind the trees.

Is David here? Is this a story he's telling me? Am I dreaming one of his stories? Let me be in it. Let me ride out into the story on Sorrow, with the three knights, the three friends who went out into the world at the end of the river to find something else, something more. New adventures. Take me there, out of this. Rescue me from my dark tower. Tell me the story. Tell me that one.

Fade out.

In the dark.

Roberts You wait! Do you hear?! I'm telling you! You've had it! All of you! You're gunna get done good and proper! You wait! You'll see. You bloody bastards! I hope your knobs rot off! I hope something horrible happens to you. Yea. Get you. Get you when you least expect it, when you've forgotten, really happy, somethin'll come and get you. Get you back for this. Rip your guts out. I hope a girder drops on your head and splatters you! You'll all die horrible. No you won't, you'll live horrible, for months, in agony, with horrible nightmares. You'll see me. I'll come to you in the night and scare you shitless. Do you hear? You're all gunna die! Dead men! You're all dead, do you hear? Eh? Fallon! You've had it. Marshall. You're dead. Carey? Fairy! Oi! Are you listening? Eh? Oi!

The bastards have buggered off and left me. Bastards!

Scene Eight

Scott's house. Today. Afternoon.

Melanie   I'll go out with who I want! What's the matter with him? He's your friend, isn't he? Was. You've got a bloody cheek telling me what to do.

Scott   Just don't bring him round here.

Melanie   I will if I want. Anyway, you're never here.

Scott   No, and when I am, I've got her bloody here.

Melanie   Just go if you're going.

Scott   I'm going. (*To* **Stella**.) Never bloody say anything, just sit in a corner and look at me.

Stella   What do you want me to say?

Scott   Nothing. I don't want you to say anything. I don't even want to see you, but I have to put up with you here, looking. Can't come in to me own house without you're looking at me.

Melanie   Get out, then.

Stella   What have I done? Just tell me what I've done.

Scott   What do you want from me?

Stella   Nothing.

Scott   Well, leave me alone, then.

Melanie   She's my friend, not yours.

Scott   I know what you're all about, don't worry. You two, getting together. I know what you're up to.

Melanie   What?

Scott   Well, it won't work.

Melanie   What?

Scott   Scheming things behind me back. I know what you're up to.

Melanie   We're not scheming anything.

Scott   No. No, of course not, course you're not. Just leave me out of things, alright? I'll do what I want and you do what you want. Alright?

Melanie   You're pathetic.

Scott   Yea?

Melanie   You need help.

Scott   Sod off.

Melanie   I mean it. You're bloody nuts.

Scott   Yea, I know.

Melanie   (*to* **Stella**) I used to like my brother, you know? He was alright. Kind. Caring. Popular. Used to have friends. Christ knows where he went. He's a shit now.

Pause.

Scott   You know nothing.

Melanie   I know I used to like you.

Scott   Well, I'm sorry for that. All change now, eh? What I was, what I am. This is me now. All grown up. And you're still so sweet and innocent.

Melanie   Get lost.

Scott   Aren't you? Like a virgin.

Melanie   Yes.

Scott   I was once. Sweet and innocent.

Stella   What are you looking at me for?

Melanie   Go away, Scott. Go on out if you're going.

Scott   I'm a man now.

Melanie   Could have fooled me.

Scott   Man of the world.

Melanie   Yea?

Scott   Experienced in life and love.

Melanie   Oh yea?

Scott   Definitely. (*To* **Stella**.) Taught me things you know nothing about.

Stella   Who? What are you on about?

Melanie   What the hell are you on about?

Scott   You're alright, Mel. You're alright. Take care of yourself.

Stella   Are you saying you were seeing somebody else when you were seeing me? Who?

Scott   Does it matter?

Stella   Who?

Scott   You know.

Stella   I don't know!

Scott   Think about it.

Stella   What?

Scott   You know.

Stella   I don't know!

Pause.

You liar.

Scott   Go home and ask her.

Stella   You liar! You bloody evil lying bastard!

Scott   You know.

Fade out.

Scene Nine

Christine's *flat. Today. Early evening.*

Eddie If I've got to take you down the station missen, and put you on the train, I'll do it. One way ticket. You got it?

Tommy You can try.

Eddie I mean it.

Tommy What do you think I'm gonna do?

Eddie I know what you're up to.

Tommy What?

Eddie Think about me. Think about Christine.

Tommy What am I going to do?

Eddie Forget it. I'm telling you. Anyway, he'll get what's coming to him without your help.

Tommy You believe that, do you?

Eddie Yes.

Tommy What, we all get what's coming to us for what we've done?

Eddie One way or another, it all works itself out. In this life or the next.

Tommy Bollocks.

Eddie I wish I'd never shown you that certificate.

Tommy Well, you did.

Eddie It could mean anything. Not what you think it means.

Tommy No?

Eddie Anything could have caused it.

Tommy Yea, like one clout too many. What else, at fifty-one? Eh?

Eddie You don't know that.

Tommy Eddie, you know as well as I do. I know where he's living. I know where he drinks. I know the streets he staggers home. I'm going to get him.

Eddie Everybody knows you're in town. People know Spawnail lived with our Mam. You don't need to be Inspector fucking Morse.

Tommy   Do they know what kind of a life Mam had with him inside that house?

Eddie   They know what he's like. They know you hate him.

Tommy   Who?

Eddie   Your mates. David Marshall for a start.

Tommy   He's not going to say anything.

Chris   You've got it all worked out, haven't you?

Tommy   He was happy to smack him with a shovel before you came along.

Chris   You want to finish up put away for good? Is that what you want? Got to go and live up to it all the way, haven't you? When you're looking at a cell wall for ten years at least you'll have the satisfaction of knowing everybody out there thinks you're the man.

Eddie   Yea, alright, Chris.

Chris   (*to* **Tommy**) You're pathetic.

Eddie   You think he's not getting back what he deserves already?

Tommy   How?

Eddie   Why do you think he spends all his time pissed out of his head? And you want to put him out of his misery? Let him walk about and feel bad forever, let the twat walk the world forever and remember what he's done.

Tommy   He doesn't feel anything.

Eddie   Well, make him feel it, then. Let him know what you know. Stick him somewhere till he's sober, so he knows what's going on. Tell him about how she died. Let it sink in. He can't hit you now. Frighten 'im, tell him you'll get him when he least expects it, when he's happy again, knocking some other woman about for love. Tell him you'll get him then. Let him worry about it. Let him go and think he's got to be looking over his shoulder all his life. That's how to get him. What satisfaction is there in doing him there and then? No, make it last. Let the maggot squirm.

Tommy   Put my foot on his face and squash the greasy git, that's what I'll do.

Chris   Listen to him. (*To* **Tommy**.) What's the matter with you?

Tommy   It's nothing to do with you!

Eddie   Yea, alright.

Tommy   (*to* **Chris**) What do you know? What do you fucking know?

Eddie   Leave it!

Chris   That's it. I don't have to put up with this. Get him out. Get him out of my flat.

Eddie   Your flat?

Chris   (*to* **Tommy**) Go on, get out! Get your stuff and get out. Find somebody else to ponce off.

Eddie   Wait a minute.

Tommy   Don't worry, I'm not stopping here.

Chris   No, you're not.

Tommy   Cow.

Eddie   Eh!

Tommy   It's her, int it? Her you're bothered about, not me. What you listening to her for?

Eddie   Shut it.

Tommy   (*to* **Chris**) You've really got your hooks into him, haven't you?

Eddie *goes for him.*

Fucking Derby and Joan.

Eddie *smacks him. They fight.*

Chris   Stop it! Stop it!

Eddie *backs off.* **Tommy** *is hurt.*

Tommy   He likes beating people up, didn't you know? Didn't you know that about him? Gets it from me Dad.

Eddie   Alright, Tommy, alright. Go on, get your bloody gear and get out. But I'm telling you, if anybody comes knocking on that door and starts giving me aggravation about you, I'll fucking find you myself before they do.

Tommy   Yea?

Eddie   Yea. Now get lost. Go on, get out.

Chris *and* **Eddie** *watch him collect his things.*

Tommy   See you.

Eddie   Yea, see you.

Tommy *goes. Pause.*

Chris   Eddie, we had to.

Eddie   Leave it.

Chris   I know, but I can't have him –

Eddie   Leave it!

Fade out.

Scene Ten

A Pub. Today. Evening. **Roberts** *is sat with a finished pint.* **Scott** *comes over with two pints, sits.*

Scott   For old times' sake. For Auld Lang Syne.

Roberts   Cheers.

Scott   How long you got left, then?

Roberts   I go back this weekend.

Scott   It's alright, then?

Roberts   Great. (*Pause.*) Tough, like.

Scott   Yea. (*Pause.*) You got some good mates there, then?

Roberts   Yea, real good. But then mates get killed, don't they?

Scott   How long you signed up for?

Roberts   Full stretch.

Scott   Bloody hell. (*Pause.*) So if you had to go somewhere . . .

Roberts   What?

Scott   You know, you wouldn't have second thoughts, if you had to, like, kill somebody?

Roberts *just looks at him.*

Well at least you've done what you wanted.

Roberts   Yea.

Scott   That's something. (*Pause.*) You're alright, you.

Roberts   You what?

Scott   You're alright.

Roberts   You pissed?

Scott   No, I mean it. You're alright. You could have spragged.

Roberts   You what?

Scott   You could have had us all done. We could have been well in trouble.

Roberts   When?

Scott   That day. That day we left you.

Roberts   Oh. Then.

Scott   You're . . . you see? You don't even – It's forgotten isn't it?

Roberts   Yea.

Scott   That's what I never . . . you never spragged. We deserved it. We deserved trouble but you never gave us any.

Roberts   No.

Scott   Why not?

Roberts   You weren't worth it.

Scott   We shouldn't have done it.

Roberts   No.

Scott   No, I mean it. It was a bad thing. I did a bad thing. I know it was. I never . . . I always wanted to say sorry, you know? Never got round to it.

Roberts   So you give it nearly three years and buy me a pint.

Scott   Yea. I know.

Roberts   Why?

Scott   I know it sounds . . . I'm not saying sorry to – It's too late for that. I know that.

Roberts   You what?

Scott   It's not you . . . You see, saying sorry to you, it doesn't fix it, does it?

Roberts   Eh?

Scott   It doesn't make it all right, does it? You know? I knew that day what we did was wrong. I knew, like, something, something else knew it was wrong. Not just you. You know what I mean?

Roberts   No.

Scott   Something else, watching me. Telling me. I'd get it all back. It would all come back to me and worse. You see?

Roberts   No. What are you on about?

Scott   David. Tommy too, maybe. He left. He knew. But where can you go? It follows you wherever, doesn't it?

Roberts   What does?

Scott   Choosing its time. I never expected it was going to be like this.

Roberts   Yea, well. Thanks for the pint. I've got to get off. Early start. Do a ten-miler before breakfast.

He goes.

Fade out.

Scene Eleven

The hospital. Midnight. **Elaine**'s *bedside.* **Tommy** *is sat, his face in a mess from the fight with* **Eddie**.

Tommy   I went to find him. Tell him what I thought of him. I was going to sort him. I thought I'd find somebody I wanted to sort for good. If he'd have laughed at me, smirked, tried to hit me again . . . it would have been easy. I could have done it easy, but he didn't do any of that. Didn't even turn away in shame or whatever. Just took it. Looking at me. Dead eyes. He was already dead, you know? Nothing. Nothing going on. Eddie was right. He was already . . . somebody else had done it for me. Mam had already done it for me, got in his head, started killing him slow, from the inside out. She didn't need me to do it for her.

They must have had something going for 'em, between 'em, eh? You can't look like he looked and not have once felt something for somebody.

I couldn't even do him for me. For what he did to me. For years I've wanted to kill him and then when I'm there, the chance to do it, I don't want to any more. Like, I've grown up to meet him grown up and settle it, and I can't because he's got past being grown up, growing back down again to old. Little again. A little old man before his time. Bent. Like killing a baby. It's all in there, what he's done, but it's all turned to mush. His brain is already mush without me making it mush. I wanted to but she'd already done it for me.

Dave *appears.*

Dave   Tommy?

Tommy   Oh, eh up, David.

Dave   What happened to you?

Tommy   I'm alright. Bit of a fight. They fixed me up downstairs, so I thought I'd come up. What you doing here at this time?

Dave   It's my weekend late night shift. (*To* **Elaine**.) Isn't it? (*To* **Tommy**.) No, my Mam's here during the day. I do the night shift at weekends. I've been out with Melanie, just took her home. Walked up. (*To* **Elaine**.) Tommy to see you, eh? Your old boyfriend.

Tommy   Eh?

Dave   She was going to marry you one day.

Tommy   Oh yea.

Dave   She was about six when she told everybody, remember?

Tommy   Yea.

Dave   So what happened, then?

Tommy   I just walked out of a pub and into a fight. It weren't about anything. They just wanted to sort me out.

Dave   They did.

Tommy   Yea. Put two of 'em down before they got me down. Somebody brought me up here in a car. Soon as I fell out she was off. Didn't even get the chance to say thanks. (*To* **Elaine**.) Trust me, eh, princess? The old scoundrel. (*Pause.*) You could bleed to death in this place before you get seen to. Sitting there ages. So I thought I'd come up here. Didn't think they'd let me. Told 'em I was her cousin.

Melanie *rushes in. Stops when she sees* **Tommy**.

What? What's up?

Melanie   I . . . David . . . I'm sorry. I had to see you.

Dave   Why, what's happened?

Melanie   I didn't know what else to do.

Tommy   I'll get off.

Dave   Wait a minute. What's – ?

Melanie   I'm sorry.

Tommy   I'll er . . .

Dave   Yea. Yea. Oh, this is Melanie. Tommy.

Tommy   Hi.

Dave   What's up?

Melanie   It's Scott.

Dave   What? What's he done?

Melanie   Oh, David. I . . . David.

Dave   What?

Melanie   He's gone. He's going to do something. I know he is.

Dave   What?

Melanie   He's got it into his head it's all he can do now.

Dave   What?

Melanie   He wouldn't come in the house. Chucking bricks up at my window. Made me go out into the yard. He wouldn't come in. Just wanted to see me.

Dave   What did he say?

Melanie   Kept going on about some woman. Some woman he's been seeing. Been giving him lessons, he said.

Dave   Lessons?

Melanie   Driving lessons. David . . . he said . . . it was him.

Dave   What was?

Melanie   He did it.

Dave   What?

Melanie   This.

Dave   You what?

Melanie   What's he going to do? I said see David. See him. See the police. Tell them. But he won't. He wants to –

Dave   It was Scott did this?

Melanie   What can we do? David? David!

Dave   Is that what you're saying?

Melanie   He's going to kill himself!

Dave   Is that what you're saying?!

Melanie   Yes. Listen. My Dad's downstairs. He brought me in the car. I haven't said anything only . . . I couldn't. I just said . . . he thinks I'm here to see you, because of Elaine. I couldn't tell him. I couldn't tell him. I let him think it was because of Elaine. I let him think he was bringing me because she . . .

Dave   Oh, Jesus. Oh, Jesus. Scott? Scott?

Melanie   Listen to me! What are we going to do? We've got to find him. David, help me.

Dave   I'll find him. I'll give him a push if he can't do it himself.

Melanie   David, don't. Don't be –

Dave   All this time. All this time.

Tommy   Wait a minute, just wait on.

Dave   Jesus.

Tommy   Stop a minute! Listen –

Dave   Jesus!

Tommy   Listen, just shut up, just listen to me a minute.

Dave   What do you know? What do you know, eh? My sister. My sister. He never stopped. He never did anything. He just left her at the side of the road.

Tommy   You've got to get the police out looking for him. Tell them what's gone on.

Dave   No.

Tommy   Yes.

Dave   If he can't go to them, if he can't walk in there and tell them . . . let him do what he's going to do.

Tommy   You don't want that.

Dave   Oh yes I do.

Tommy   No you don't.

Dave   No, too easy. Find him. Let him know what this – I want him to know first. I want him to hear me first. Then he can – then I'll save him the bother.

Tommy   (*to* **Melanie**) Ring the police. Tell your Dad.

Dave   No.

Tommy   Let them find him. Then you can see him. Then you can let him know.

Dave   You wouldn't if it were you.

Tommy   It's not me.

Dave   Would you? You wouldn't. You'd want the same. Sort it out yourself. Wouldn't you? Wouldn't you?!

Tommy   Listen, David, I know what –

Dave   You know nothing.

Tommy   Why do you think he's gone off to do this? Eh? You think he feels nothing? You think you telling him what he's done, letting him know how you feel, smacking him . . . you think he can feel any worse?

Dave   Yes.

Tommy   He can't feel any worse if he's doing this.

Melanie   Please, David. Please.

Tommy   (*to* **Melanie**) Ring the police. Tell your Dad. Are you sure about this?

Melanie   I think so.

Tommy   Never mind think! Are you sure?

Melanie   Yes.

Tommy Ring 'em, then.

Melanie Can't we find him? Don't you know where he might be? Can't we look first?

Tommy Why?

Melanie I can't tell this to my Dad. I can't. Not now.

Dave I'll tell him. I'll tell him what his son's done.

Tommy Wait. Wait a minute. It's not for you to tell him.

Dave Why not?

Tommy It's not.

Dave (*to* **Melanie**) You come, then. Come on, we'll both go down.

Melanie Wait. Wait. What if. . . ? What if he. . . ? It's all mixed up. He's saying this . . . maybe . . . if we find him first . . . if you tell them now and tell the police, it'll kill them. My Mam and Dad would . . . Can't we find him? Can't we get him to go to the police? That's what I want. I don't want this. You're not doing it this way. If Scott sees the police he might panic and do it. If we find him, if we find him first, talk to him, find out . . . let him go to them himself, or take him, then tell my parents tomorrow . . . it won't be such a shock. If he sees the police he could. . . . Please. We've got to do it like this. Please.

Tommy What exactly did he say? Come on. Did he say anything at all about where he might be going?

Melanie No. I don't know. He could be anywhere.

Tommy What did he say? Come on.

Melanie He said he'd seen somebody.

Tommy Who?

Melanie I don't know. Something about when he was younger. Something about where it all started. Somebody called . . . you were there. He said you two were there.

Tommy Who? When? What was his name?

Melanie I can't remember.

Dave Roberts.

Dave *makes a move.*

Melanie What? David! Where are you going? Where is he?

Tommy   O.K. Me and you, David. Me and you'll go. (*To* **Melanie**.) You sort this out with your Dad.

Melanie   No, I want to come with you.

Dave   No.

Melanie   I'm coming with you!

Tommy   Sort out downstairs with your Dad first.

Melanie   What do I say?

Dave   You got yourself into it, you get yourself out.

Melanie   What can I say? Just a . . . David, wait! Let me think of something first! David! Wait for me!

Dave *and* **Tommy** *go.*

Fade out.

Scene Twelve

Along the river.

Scott *watches the young trio.*

Young Scott   I don't want to get old.

Young Dave   Me neither.

Young Tommy   They ought to make a law so you get put down when you're thirty.

Young Dave   Yea.

Young Scott   Yea. All they go on about is when they were young anyway.

Young Dave   I know. Boring.

Young Scott   They don't do anything, just sit around. Go to work, come home, sit around, watch telly, go to bed.

Young Dave   I'd rather be dead. It should be if you get boring you get put down.

Young Scott   Yea.

Young Dave   I mean, 'cos not all of 'em's boring. Some of 'em's alright.

Young Tommy   Not many.

Young Dave   I know, but some.

Young Tommy   Who?

Young Dave   Who's that dead old bloke what sings?

Young Scott   Who?

Young Dave   There's a few of 'em. They're all dead old but they still have a good time. Him what dives about and dances.

Young Scott   You mean Rolling Stones.

Young Dave   Yea, that's 'em.

Young Tommy   My Mam likes them.

Young Scott   Yea, but they're singers, aren't they? They're in a band. You don't get boring in a band.

Young Tommy   I bet they do off stage.

Young Dave   They have all them women what come to see their concerts in their dressing rooms. That's what keeps 'em feeling young.

Young Scott   Do you reckon?

Young Dave   Yea.

Young Scott   They must be mad.

Young Dave   Who?

Young Scott   Them women, doing that. Like kissing a dead body.

Young Tommy   Yea but some women like old men. Anyway it keeps 'em writing songs and that, keeps 'em able to write about sex, drugs and rock and roll.

Young Scott   Do you think they still do it?

Young Dave   What?

Young Scott   Have sex?

Young Tommy   No.

Young Dave   No. Too old. They just have women about to help 'em remember.

Young Scott   You reckon?

Young Dave   Yea.

Young Scott   Yea. I think my Dad stopped doing it when he were twenty. My Mam says he did, anyway.

Young Tommy   Twenty?

Young Scott   Yea.

Young Tommy   I've got loads of time to do it, then.

Young Scott   Years.

Young Dave   Depends when you start. If you don't do it till you're eighteen . . .

Young Tommy   Yea. Our Eddie says when he starts, he's going to do it with one woman from every country in the world.

Young Scott   How many's that?

Young Tommy   About fifteen.

Young Dave   What, even Russia?

Young Tommy   What's up with that?

Young Dave   They're all big and hairy.

Young Tommy No they're not.

Young Scott That's Eskimos.

Young Tommy Yea. Doing it in an igloo.

Young Dave Them Borneo women, bones through their noses. Them things they have in their lips.

Young Tommy Yea. You wouldn't be able to snog, would you?

Young Dave They don't snog.

Young Tommy What do they do, then?

Young Scott They do snog, then, 'cos it's a bit of wood that they can take out and it leaves a big hole in their lips. The men put their tongues through the hole.

Dave *and* **Tommy** *pretend puking.*

Scott *begins to sing a Rolling Stones song.* **Young Dave** *and* **Young Tommy** *freeze.* **Young Scott** *picks up a stick, begins to play guitar with it and sing along.* **Young Tommy** *slowly gets up and moves off, followed by* **Young Dave**. *When the song finishes,* **Young Scott** *takes out a knife and begins to make a point on the stick.*

Tommy *appears.*

Tommy (*calling off*) David! (*Pause.*) David! He's here! Scott? Scott, you alright? Scott?

Young Scott *gets up, leaving the stick and the knife. Goes off.*

Scott Tommy?

Tommy We've been looking all along the river.

Scott What for?

Tommy You.

Scott Why?

Tommy Why do you think?

Scott When did you come home?

Tommy Last week. You had us worried.

Scott I'm alright.

Dave *appears.*

Tommy Have you taken anything?

Scott Eh?

Tommy Have you taken anything? Pills, or anything?

Scott No. Pills? Why?

Tommy   We know what you've done.

Scott   What?

Tommy   We've seen Melanie. Melanie said you told her what you'd done.

Scott   Did I?

Tommy   Yes.

Scott   I must have done.

Dave   So?

Scott   Sorry?

Dave   You bastard.

Dave *goes for him, gets hold of him, belts him.* **Scott** *goes down.*

Tommy   Leave him! Leave him!

Dave   Get up! Get up!

Tommy   Don't, David.

Scott *gets up.* **Dave** *belts him again.* **Scott** *goes down,* **Dave** *lays in to him.* **Tommy** *tries to stop him, but can't do much with his injured arm so shoulders him away.* **Dave** *belts* **Tommy**, **Tommy** *manages to put him down.*

Dave   What am I supposed to do? What else am I supposed to do?

Scott *picks up the pointed stick, puts the point into his eye socket, rests the other end on the ground.*

Go on, then, do it! Do it! Fucking coward can't even do it. Just said it for sympathy, wants us all to feel sorry for him. Fucking do it, go on!

Young Scott, **Young Tommy** *and* **Young Dave** *appear.*

Young Dave   I'll kill you if you've lost it.

Young Scott   I haven't lost it.

Young Dave   Where is it, then?

Young Scott   It's here somewhere.

Young Dave   You'd better find it.

Young Scott   It's only a knife.

Young Dave   It's my best knife.

Young Scott   I'll buy you another.

Young Dave   It's my Dad's. He dunt know I've got it. He'll kill me.

Tommy *finds it.*

Young Tommy   It's here.

Young Dave   Give me it.

Young Tommy   Here.

Young Scott   See?

Young Dave   You're not borrowing it any more.

Young Scott   I don't want to, don't worry. Nearly crying over a knife.

Young Dave   I wa'nt.

Young Scott   You were. (*To* **Tommy**.) Wa'nt he?

Young Tommy   Yea.

Young Dave   Get lost, both of you.

Young Scott   You big puff, crying.

Young Dave   I'm off home.

Young Scott   Puff.

Young Dave   I thought we were friends?

Young Scott   Not to puffs, I'm not.

Young Dave   Stop saying that!

Young Scott   Puff!

Young Dave   Do you want a fight or something?

Young Scott   Why, do you?

Young Dave   You're asking for one.

Young Scott   Am I?

Young Dave   Are you?

Young Scott   I'm not scared of you.

Young Dave   I'm not scared of you.

Young Tommy   Go on, have a fight. I wouldn't stand for that, Dave, what he called you.

Young Dave   Shut up, you.

Young Tommy   Come on, Scott.

Young Scott   You shut up.

Young Tommy   Are you having a fight or what?

Young Dave   I might.

Young Scott   Yea, we might. What's it got to do with you?

Young Tommy   You're both scared. Come on, I'll be referee. Boxing or wrestling?

Young Dave   He can choose.

Young Scott   You choose. I'm not bothered.

Young Dave   I'm not.

Young Tommy   Boxing, then. Scott?

Young Scott   It's up to him.

Young Tommy   Dave?

Young Dave   I'm not bothered.

Young Tommy   Come on, make your minds up. You're both scared.

Young Dave   Just 'cos you're always fighting.

Young Scott   Yea.

Young Tommy   I could fight both of you together.

Young Dave   So?

Young Tommy   One hand tied behind me back.

Young Dave   I don't want to.

Young Tommy   Coward.

Young Dave   Get lost. He's the coward.

Young Scott   I'm not.

Young Tommy   I'll fight the winner of you two.

Young Scott   You don't fight fair, anyway. You cheat.

Young Tommy   I don't.

Young Dave   Yea, he does.

Young Scott   I know.

Young Dave   We don't fight cheats.

Young Scott   No, we don't.

Young Tommy   You do if I make you.

Young Scott   Anyway, I'm not allowed to fight any more because I've got double O.

Young Tommy   You what?

Young Scott   I have, then, you ask me Mam.

Young Tommy   What's that?

Young Scott   Double O blood.

Young Tommy What's that?

Young Scott It's a special blood group. It's rare. If I get cut they can't get any more. It's what kings have.

Young Dave You what?

Young Scott My blood won't stop bleeding. It doesn't go dry after a bit like everybody elses. It's what kings have.

Young Dave You liar.

Young Scott I'm not. It's got blue in it.

Young Dave Prove it.

Young Scott No.

Young Dave Go on, cut your finger with my knife.

Young Scott No, I'll bleed to death.

Young Dave You won't.

Young Scott We're too far from the hospital.

Young Tommy Do it, or we won't believe you.

Young Scott I don't care.

Young Tommy You're a big liar, then. Just 'cos you're scared to fight.

Young Scott I'm not.

Young Tommy Come on, let's get him. Let's cut him and see.

Young Tommy *and* **Young Dave** *grab* **Young Scott**, *they tussle.* **Young Dave** *gets hold of the knife.*

Young Scott Don't Dave! Don't Dave! Dave!

Young Dave Look. I dare do it.

He makes a pin prick in his finger.

Look.

He gives the knife to **Young Tommy**.

Young Tommy I dare.

He cuts across his palm.

Look.

He gives the knife to **Young Scott**.

Come on, blood brothers.

Young Tommy *and* **Young Dave** *hold hands.*

Young Scott You puffs.

Young Dave   Come on, then.

Young Scott   I can't.

Young Tommy   You can't be a blood brother till you do.

Young Scott   It won't stop.

Young Dave   Prove it.

Young Tommy   Suck it, then. It'll all go back then.

Young Dave   Yea, it'll keep going round.

Young Scott   I can't keep sucking it forever, can I? What about when I'm asleep?

Young Tommy   We don't believe you.

Young Dave   No, we don't believe you.

Young Tommy   If you've got kings' blood, you've got to prove it. Come on.

Young Dave   Come on. Mingle your blood. Let's be blood brothers. Do it!

Young Scott *takes the knife.*

Dave   Do it!

Tommy *moves to* **Scott**, *gets hold of him by the hair, pulls him up, grabs the stick.*

Tommy   Say something! Say something to him! Come on! Say something!

Scott   Alright, alright.

Tommy   Go on, then.

Scott   Give me the knife.

Tommy   What knife?

Scott   Give me the knife.

Tommy   What fucking knife? Scott!

He pulls his hair. **Scott** *cries out.* **Tommy** *drags him over to* **David**, *sets him down facing him.*

Tell him. Tell David what you've done. Do it! Tell him what you've done. Tell him how that makes you feel. Do it!

Young Scott *cuts his palm.*

Young Dave   Let's have a look. He's done it.

Young Tommy   Good one. Good one. You're a bleeder.

Young Scott   Sometimes it stops. It's only sometimes it keeps bleeding.

Young Dave   I'm not mixing with that. I don't want what he's got. Yeeagh.

Young Scott   Come on, I've done it now.

Young Dave   No, thanks.

Young Scott   Tommy. You.

Young Tommy   No.

Young Scott   What am I going to do with it, then?

He makes to touch them with his hand, they back off. He gets **Young Dave**.

You've got it now. You've got my lurgy.

He chases **Young Tommy** *off.*

Young Dave   Yeeah.

He spits on it, rubs it on his trousers.

I'm off to the river and wash it off.

He goes off.

Scott   I'm sorry. I'm sorry.

Pause.

Dave   What do you want me to say?

Pause.

Tommy   Come on, Scott, let's go.

Scott   Listen.

Tommy   What?

Scott   Can you hear the river?

Tommy   No.

Scott   No. You think you would at night.

Tommy   Come on, Scott. This is . . . Let's go, yeah? Come on, you can't stay here.

Scott   Can't run away from it.

Tommy   No.

Scott   Are you back now?

Tommy   No. In the morning I'm –

Scott   I saw Roberts tonight.

Tommy   Yeah?

Scott   Remember Roberts? The kid we put down the lime kiln. He was alright about it. (*Pause.*) This place. It knows everything, doesn't it? Remembers everything. You know what I mean? Stores it in the rocks, the trees. Even things not said, just thought. Me. You. Dave. We're all here. Was that us? I mean, it's like it happened to somebody else. But it wasn't. It was me. Who did I become?

Tommy   Listen. You've told. You've said something. You've moved on. You're not where you were today. It's a start. You can face it. You've moved on. Going back . . . doesn't matter whether it was good or bad. It still hurts, doesn't help with now.

We're all guilty of . . . something . . . things we say, things we do. You have to . . . You can't say what's going to happen. You don't know what – You've just got to get on with it, Scott.

Scott   You know what I want? Right now, she wakes up out of it. She's alright. She's out of it. She's come round. She's up and speaking. She wants to see me. She keeps saying my name, because my face is all she remembers. And we go and she's there, and she says 'It's all right, Scott. It's all right. I know, but I'm back now. And everybody's alright. Everybody's happy.' And we're mates again, and you say you're not going away any more.

Tommy   Yea.

Dave   What you want and what you get . . .

Scott   I know.

Pause. Voices over.

Stella   Please, Scott, talk to me. Why won't you talk to me?

Scott   Go home, Stella.

Stella   Scott.

Scott   Go home. I can't –

Stella   Scott, don't . . .

Scott   I don't want to see you any more. Alright? What do I have to do, throw you out?

Pause.

Tommy   You've really got your hooks into him, haven't you? Fucking Derby and Joan.

Chris   You're pathetic!

Eddie   Alright, Tommy, alright. Go on. Get your bloody gear and get out.

Pause.

Melanie I used to like my brother, you know? He was alright. Kind. Caring. Popular. Used to have friends. Christ knows where he went. He's a shit now.

Pause.

Dave I'll find him. I'll give him a push if he can't do it himself.

Melanie David, don't be –

Dave All this time. All this time!

Pause. The voices have gone.

Dave I'm going.

Tommy Yea. Scott?

Scott Yea.

*They don't move. The lights begin to fade and we hear **Elaine**'s voice.*

Elaine Let me ride out into the story on Sorrow, with the three knights. The three friends who went out into the world at the end of the river to find something else, something more. New adventures. Take me there, out of this. Rescue me. Tell me the story. Tell me that one.

And then darkness.

Triggered by Guilt

Richard Cameron interviewed by Jim Mulligan

For eighteen years, Richard Cameron was Head of Drama in a comprehensive school, and throughout that time he wrote plays for the children he taught and for youth theatre groups. In the early '80s he entered a play for the National Student Drama Festival and won several awards, among them a Fringe First at the Edinburgh Festival and the Independent Theatre Award. This was the sign that, at 42, it was time to give up teaching and write full time. He still does workshops but his full-time occupation is writing plays for the stage though this year he has won the BBC Dennis Potter Play of the Year Award for his first venture into television.

'I spend a long time structuring my work before I write a word down. I usually spend three months on a first draft and a month on the second draft. But before that you have to get your ideas for the play. You can't just sit in front of a piece of paper and hope an idea is going to drop into your head. So I do other things, and think about characters and incidents and episodes until something crystallizes. Once a piece is structured I am fairly disciplined. I work from nine in the morning to four in the afternoon and sometimes go on into the evening.'

Almost Grown is a play that was triggered by guilt. Richard Cameron admits to being obsessed by the things people do to others and the repercussions of actions taken a long way into the past. He started off with the idea of some people in their teenage years who are cursed for something they did when they were just starting adolescence; and he pondered on how the curse might be fulfilled and if they would recognize the origin of the curse when it was fulfilled.

'In a very real sense, the play is about my guilt. I have done things I regret. But you can't go back. You can't change things which have been done. When I was a teenager, for example, I was sometimes a bully at school. Everyone was. There was a pecking order: you got bullied so you passed it on. The people I would dearly love to meet now, in my middle age, are the people I gave a hard time to, so that I could say sorry. It'll never happen, of course, so I write about it instead. In that sense, the play for me is a kind of expiation. I feel better for having written it. It helps me understand myself. This is not a unique experience. It happens to all of us.'

Richard Cameron is fascinated by childhood and the timelessness that children experience. 'Childhood features in a lot of my plays. Not that I put children into them, but the things that my characters did when they were children account for some of the behaviour and attitudes and events we see in the play. What happened to the child's concept of time? Where did it go and why can't we live in the moment as we did when we were children? Why is it that we are always obsessed by the past and the future? The older we get, the more preoccupied we are with what was and what is to come, but when you're a kid you can hold the moment. You can make it last all day, live in it, be there, and nothing else matters.'

In *Almost Grown*, we are given glimpses of different kinds of families with differing incomes and social statuses. Richard Cameron spent his childhood in a family that was hovering between working-class and lower-middle-class. His father worked on the railways and they were the only family on the estate where they lived to vote Conservative. 'We got mud slung at our door for that, and I got into a few fights because of it. In South Yorkshire, where all my plays are set, you mix with different people at school and it doesn't matter. It's only later on that you go your separate ways. I can clearly remember having friends that I thought would be friends for life and two years later I had moved on and had different friends. That is a phenomenon that fascinates me. I'd love to go back and find out what those people are doing now.'

Sexuality and violence are faced squarely in this play because they are an essential part of teenage culture. But Richard Cameron warns against taking the sexuality too seriously. Teenagers lie about their sexual experiences. They exaggerate. There is bravado, a sense of adventure and fantasy. But the violence in our society is real.

'Violence happens. That's all I can say. There's no getting away from it. I write about what I see around me. And, I have to admit, it is dramatically effective. I don't so much object to two guys slugging it out in a fight. The physical violence and the cruel words of the young are often spontaneous. It is the calculated, never-ending, demoralizing mental cruelty that adults inflict on others that is, to me, much more of an outrage. That kind of pain is not the ferocity of *Almost Grown*, though I have dealt with it in other plays. I suppose, if I'm honest, I have to say that I can't get away from wanting to know why we do the things we do to others.'

If violence is a fact of life, then criminality among young men is also evident in the area where Richard Cameron lives. The central action of *Almost Grown*, he asserts, is the reckless driving of Scott, which puts Dave's sister, Elaine, into a coma.

'It's not the incident itself that fascinates me; it's the ripple that affects life for generations to come. Not everything we do is as dramatic as Scott's moment of madness when he drives off, leaving Elaine, but the things we've said and done come back to haunt us. Despite all this guilt, I believe *Almost Grown* is a hopeful play in the sense that it shows us that we have to let go, move on, and live our own lives. The past is painful. We do things we regret and we can't put them right. The best we can hope for is that someone else might rectify things. We can only learn from our actions and move on.'

Richard Cameron is from Doncaster. His plays include the award-winning *The Moon's the Madonna* and *Strugglers* (both written for the National Student Drama Company) and *Can't Stand Up for Falling Down* (Edinburgh Festival, winner of the Independent Theatre Award; Hampstead Theatre, 1990; and

Hull Truck Tour, 1992). These plays have been published by Methuen. More recently *Pond Life* (a co-production with the National Theatre Studio), *Not Fade Away* and *The Mortal Ash* have premièred at the Bush Theatre in highly praised productions. Richard has also been commissioned by the West Yorkshire Playhouse.

Almost Grown

Production Notes

Setting and staging
Moving backwards and forwards in time over recent years, the play is set somewhere along a river bank: in houses, a flat, a backyard, a pub, and a hospital. The set cannot be realistic if the action is to be fluid. There are, however, important elements. The exterior 'river' scene is dominant. It might include a patch of grass with trees, with a lime-kiln in the background. The interiors should be as simple as possible, with perhaps nothing more than a suggestion of an interior superimposed on the landscape.

Music and sound will help to create the atmosphere. The title comes from a song by Chuck Berry. It suggests that the play is about transition from youth to adulthood – what we lose, what we gain. The opening music is 'I know an old lady who swallowed a fly'. There are several sound effects, such as the river and the sound of a car screeching.

Time and place come out of what is said and shouldn't be specifically signalled. The play presents a kind of puzzle, which is eventually worked out in the last scene, thus bringing together the various strands of the story. The play was written with Yorkshire accents in mind, because that is the way Richard Cameron imagined it, but it can be set anywhere.

Casting
A cast of twelve, aged 10–20. Elaine is probably the most difficult character to play because her experiences are all shown through the trance state of coma – a dream, which has no obvious reference to reality. The actors playing Young Scott, David, and Tommy cannot also play their older counterparts, and so careful casting is required here.

Questions

1. What sorts of violence occur in the play? Can any of it be justified? If it can, how do we present it on stage?

2. How does the theme of retribution manifest itself and which characters believe in it?

3. The story that is told is bigger than the scenes which we see. Which characters and scenes exist *outside* what is shown on stage?

4. What incidents occur in the play that cannot be put right? How might we express this finality?

5. All the characters are credible, but the characters themselves do not always tell the truth about themselves and about events. Identify where

this happens in the play. For instance, what exactly is the relationship Stella has with Tommy and with Scott?

Exercises

1. Create a 'storyboard', i.e. a series of drawings depicting 'freeze frame' pictures of key moments in the story, which take into account the flash-backs and flash-forwards in time.

2. Melanie, the most sympathetic character, has come to terms with the events which alter her relationship with Scott, David, and Elaine. Discuss to what varying degrees other characters cope with changing situations, and explore these changes through improvisation.

3. Perhaps the most surprising thing about the play is Roberts' 'forgiving'. Discuss how what one says and believes when fifteen, in a moment of crisis, can be totally different when one is, say, eighteen. What elements create this change? Again, explore through improvisation.

4. Chris says of Tommy, 'He brings it all back, doesn't he? Something about him puts me on edge'. While Tommy says of himself, 'You get a reputation you have to keep living up to.' What other comments are made which give insight to any one of the characters? 'Hot-seat' each of the actors in relation to the characters they play, with the group asking questions arising either from the text, or from situations explored in improvisation.

5. Set up improvisations based on questions 1–5 above, with the aim of 'filling out' the environment (and relationships) amongst which the characters live.

Suzy Graham-Adriani
Director/Producer for BT National Connections

The Ice Palace

Lucinda Coxon

(adapted from Is-Slottet, *a novel by Tarjei Vesaas*
translated from the Norwegian by Elizabeth Rokkan, and published by Peter Owen Ltd)

Characters

Siss   *11 years (F)*
Unn   *11 years (F)*
Mother   *(of Siss)*
Father   *(of Siss)*
Auntie   *(Unn's)*
Teacher   *(M/F)*
Torill   *11 years (F)*
Helle   *11 years (F)*
Inge   *11 years (F)*
Selma   *11 years (F)*
Erik   *11 years (M)*
Klaus   *11 years (M)*
Mats   *11 years (M)*
Searchers   *(minumum of five, M/F)*
Shadows   *three, M/F*
Echo   *(F)*

Stage directions are suggestions to help provide a picture for the reader. They should be deemed optional in rehearsal/production.

In the text, the scenes are clearly divided. I would not expect those divisions to be anything like as distinct in production.

Staging
I have assumed an upper and lower stage level and also an area dominated by verticals to represent the dredging poles, the forest and the ice palace.

Preset: on the stage, a model village with little squares of orange, glowing from within to mark the windows. The model should stay on stage throughout.

Scene One

The Forest.

Afternoon. It's dark, but there's a moon that casts long shadows.
Siss *starts to walk on the spot facing front, full of purpose.*

Siss   The most important thing to remember when making your way through the woods in the dark . . .

Shadow 1   especially on a very very cold afternoon in late Autumn

Shadow 2   afternoon but already dark

Shadow 3   bundled up against the frost

Siss   is never, never, never, never . . . to run. You can walk very fast, but it must be a walk. One foot on the ground at all times. Otherwise the things at the side of the road can get you. Likewise, you must not look round if you hear a suspicious noise . . .

Shadow 1   A young white forehead, boring through the darkness

Siss   but keep your eyes focused on the path ahead . . .

Shadow 2   an eleven-year-old girl . . .

Siss   and your mind fixed on your destination . . .

Shadow 3   Siss!

Then **Siss's Mother** *calls.*

Mother   Siss! Why, Siss!

Siss *is irritated. Keeps walking.*

Siss   Yes, what is it now?

Mother   You're so excited you forgot your mittens!

Siss's Mother *flaps a pair of mittens.*

Siss   Oh . . .

Mother   Your little hands'll freeze right off!

Siss *keeps walking on the spot. Her* **Mother** *pushes the mittens onto her hands.* **Siss's Father** *appears.*

Father   She'd forget her head if it were loose!

Mother   She's just excited.

Father   And maybe a little afraid!

Siss   Am not.

Mother   Afraid of what?

Father   Of the dark.

Siss   I'm not a baby.

There is a loud crack from the lake. **Siss** *flinches.*

Father   It's only the ice on the lake.

Siss   I know that.

Mother   Should one of us go with you? I could fetch my coat and . . .

Siss   No! I'm going by myself. I'll be alright.

Mother   But . . .

Father   It's the main road most of the way.

Siss   See.

Mother   So long as you're sure . . .

Father   What's this new girl's name again?

Shadows   (*whisper*) Unn, Unn, Unn!

Siss   Oh! Stop it, you're making me late!

Siss *flaps her parents away in a rage of impatience. They disappear. She resumes.*

Yes . . . keep your mind fixed on your destination. And stick to the path, because on either side is the forest and the undergrowth . . . deathly-still with everything that might be alive and shivering in there at the moment . . .

But while she's talking, a group of schoolchildren emerges slowly from the darkness of the forest. **Siss** *senses something, stops, listens hard, afraid.*

Do you ever get the feeling . . . that you're being watched?

The children start to whisper noisily.

All   What's the time, Mr Wolf?

Siss *spins round, terrified, screams out, her heart racing. The children complain.*

Inge   You're not supposed to look round.

Siss *laughs with relief that it's just her schoolmates.*

Siss   It's just you!

Torill   Who else would it be?

Siss   I don't know.

Helle   Now turn back.

Erik   And cover your eyes.

Siss *does so. The children whisper again and steal towards* **Siss**, *all except one,* **Unn**, *who remains silent and still.* **Siss** *strains to hear the footsteps. The breath that approaches . . .*

All   What's the time, Mr Wolf?

They stop.

Siss   One o'clock.

They move again.

All   What's the time, Mr Wolf?

Siss   Two o'clock . . .

All   What's the time, Mr Wolf?

Siss   . . . dinnertime!

She turns on the others and they scatter away, squealing with excitement. She tries to catch a couple of them but fails. Then she sees **Unn**. *Stops in her tracks.*

Siss   You're not running.

Unn   I'm not afraid.

Siss *is nonplussed.*

Siss   You have to be, it's the whole point of the game.

Unn   I'm not playing.

Siss   Oh. Are you going to play later?

Unn   No.

Siss   Why?

Unn   I can't?

Siss   Why not?

Unn   Why ask?

Siss   It might be fun . . .

Unn   I don't want to talk about it. And I don't want you to ask me again.

Siss *is taken aback.*

Siss   Sure.

Unn   I have to go now. My Aunt will worry if I'm late.

Unn *leaves.* **Siss** *watches her go, then realises that she has forgotten about her journey. Resumes walking, slightly shaken.*

Siss   Yes . . . your mind fixed . . . on your . . .

Unn *appears in the orange-lighted window of her home. Looks out for* **Siss**. **Siss** *senses it.*

your destination . . .

Siss *closes her eyes, breathes in the sensation of being watched, keeps walking. The schoolchildren run in, passing a note from hand to hand, teasing.* **Siss** *suddenly opens her eyes.*

Give me that!

Helle   'I must meet you Siss', signed 'Unn'!

Siss *chases the girl and catches the note off her, but immediately another one calls out.*

Klaus   'When can I meet you, Unn?', signed 'Siss'!

She chases him and again retrieves the note. But immediately:

Torill   'Whenever you like, Unn! You can meet me today!'

They toss the crumpled note to one another, making **Siss** *jump after it, then throw it high in the air and run away.* **Siss** *grabs the note.*

Siss   Today.

Siss *makes a secret promise sign to the invisible sender.*

After all this time of waiting and watching . . . of hide-and-seeking . . . of imagining the day when . . .

A voice cuts through the air.

Unn   Hallo, Siss.

Siss *sees* **Unn** *standing in the lighted doorway. She savours the sight. Beat.*

Siss   Hello, Unn.

They stand apart, tense for a moment. Then **Unn** *laughs and the atmosphere is playful.*

Unn   At last.

Siss   Yes.

Unn   Must've been dark.

Siss   Doesn't bother me.

Unn   Freezing cold too.

Siss   Doesn't bother me either.

Unn   You've been here before. A long time ago.

Siss   Before I knew about you.

Auntie *appears behind* **Unn**.

Auntie   Siss! Come along in quickly! It's too cold to stand out there. Come into the warm.

Unn   Come into the warm.

They follow her in.

Auntie   Now take off your things.

Siss *starts to undo her boots, watching* **Unn** *all the while.*

Do you remember how it looked when you came here before? A long time ago, now. I've seen you since then, around and about. But there was nothing to bring you back here till now. Till Unn came to live with me. I'm lucky to have her . . .

Unn   Auntie . . .

Auntie   I know, I know! I'm carrying on! Now Siss must have a hot drink to warm her up . . .

Siss *looks to* **Unn**. **Unn** *shakes her head.*

Siss   I'm really not cold, thank you.

Unn   I have my own room. We'll go there.

Auntie   Are you sure?

Unn   Are you coming?

Siss *smiles.* **Unn** *guides* **Siss** *into the room.* **Siss** *looks around – she's dreamt of this.*

Unn   Is your room bigger?

Siss   About the same.

Unn   There's no need for anything bigger.

Siss   I agree.

Unn   Please.

She points to a chair. **Siss** *sits.* **Unn** *sits on the bed. A long uncomfortable silence, then* **Unn** *gets up and locks the door.*

Siss   Why did you do that?

Unn   She might come in. I wanted us to be alone together.

Siss   Oh. Yes. Of course. At last!

Unn *sits down again.*

Unn   How old are you?

Siss   Eleven-and-a-bit.

Unn   And me.

Siss   We're the same height too.

Unn   Yes.

Beat.

Siss   Do you like it here?

Unn   My aunt's kind.

Siss   No – I meant . . . at school . . .

Unn   I don't mind it.

Siss   You get good marks!

Unn   I study hard.

Siss   Why don't you join in more?

Unn   I told you not to ask.

Siss   Sorry. I didn't mean to . . .

Unn   Don't go on about it . . .

Siss   No.

Beat.

Are you going to stay here now?

Unn *fixes her with a stare. Considers.*

Unn   I've nowhere else to go.

Beat.

Why don't you ask about my mother?

Siss   I . . . I don't know.

Unn   No?

Siss   Because I heard she died, I suppose.

Unn   She wasn't married. In case you heard that too.

Siss   Oh. No. I mean, yes.

Unn   Last Spring she fell ill. She was sick for just a week, then –

Unn *draws her finger across her throat with some relish, unsettling* **Siss**.

Siss   Sorry.

Unn   Do you know anything about my father?

Siss *shakes her head.*

Nor me. Some things mother told me. I've never seen him. He had a car.

Siss   That's nice.

Unn   Do you think?

Siss   Better than not.

Unn   I shall stay with Auntie forever now.

Siss *is happy again.*

Siss   Yes. Stay here.

Unn   Do you have brothers and sisters?

Siss   No.

Unn *smiles.*

Unn   That works out well then, doesn't it?

Siss   It means we can meet often.

Unn   We meet every day at school as it is.

Unn *laughs.*

Come over here.

Siss *hesitates.*

Unn   Come on!

Siss *goes to sit right next to* **Unn.**

I want to show you something.

Unn *slides out something from under the bed, lays it across both their laps. It has a scarf wrapped around it. As* **Siss** *watches,* **Unn** *removes the scarf.*

Siss   A mirror . . .

Unn   Look into it with me . . .

Unn *holds up the mirror, looks into it.* **Siss** *joins in. Their attention is drawn further and further into the glass. The light flickers and a dislocated sound of girls' laughter fills the room, echoes louder and louder and louder until it is no longer laughter but the sound of someone crying out . . .*

Siss *and* **Unn** *start to cry out too . . .*

The ice cracks on the lake, breaking the trance. **Unn** *and* **Siss** *push the mirror away, shaken. A moment.*

Siss   Did you know . . . about this?

Unn   Did you see it too?

Beat.

Siss   I don't suppose it was anything.

Unn   No.

Siss   But it was strange. Cover it over.

Unn *does so, puts the mirror back under the bed.*

Unn   It's gone now.

More silence, until:

Unn   I think we should take our clothes off.

Siss   Take our. . . ?

Unn   All of them. It would be fun wouldn't it?

Siss   Would it?

Siss *isn't sure, but* **Unn** *pulls off her shirt. Waits.* **Siss** *copies. Then* **Unn** *pulls off her trousers.* **Siss** *hesitates then joins in.* **Unn** *quickly pulls off her underwear and* **Siss** *is only moments behind. They stand naked. Look at one another. An extraordinary moment.*

Siss   We look the same.

There is a moment of terrible intimacy, vulnerability. Then suddenly **Unn** *is upset.*

Unn   It's too cold after all.

She picks up her clothes, starts to pull them back on.

Siss   No! Not if we jump about!

Siss *jumps up and down on the bed.*

Unn   There's a draught. Can't you feel it?

Siss   But it's quite warm here . . .

Unn   Put your clothes on, Siss . . . Now! I mean it.

Siss *is bewildered, stops bouncing. Suddenly embarrassed,* **Siss** *pulls her clothes on again.* **Unn** *looks away. When* **Siss** *is dressed:*

Siss   I don't understand.

Unn   I don't want to talk about it.

Siss   So what will we do now?

Unn   We'll think of somthing.

Siss   I hope so, otherwise I might have to go home.

Unn *looks round, makes eye contact again.*

Unn   No – don't do that . . . not yet.

Siss   I don't want to.

It's clear that **Unn***'s got to think of something to make* **Siss** *stay. Suddenly she has an idea.*

Unn Do you want to see pictures, of where I lived before?

Siss Yeah!

Unn Okay . . .

Unn *brightens, takes out a small folder . . .*

Unn Look! This is my mother.

Siss *looks.*

Siss She looks nice.

Unn *smiles.*

Unn And my father. That's his car.

Siss It's a good one.

Unn Is it?

Siss Where is he now?

Unn *shrugs.*

Unn If they knew that I don't suppose I'd have come to live here.

Siss No.

They turn a page. **Siss** *laughs.*

Ha! That's you!

Unn Yes.

Siss When you were a little baby.

Unn Can I see?

She takes the folder from **Siss**. *Looks at the picture of herself. Is quiet, until:*

Siss?

Siss Yes?

Unn There's something I want to . . .

Siss What?

Unn Tell you.

Siss Oh?

Unn Something I've never told anyone.

Siss No one?

Unn Not another living soul.

Siss   Not even your mother?

Unn   Oh no! Never.

Siss *thinks. It seems a bit scary.*

Siss   Alright then.

Unn   And if I tell you, you must swear you'll never tell.

Siss   I won't.

Unn   Are you sure you want to know?

Siss   I think so.

Unn   Swear it on our friendship, Siss.

Siss *thinks a moment, then very seriously makes the promise signal.*[1]
Unn *repeats it back to her, tries to summon the courage to speak.*
Siss *waits, nervous now of what* **Unn** *might be about to say. But* **Unn** *says nothing.*

Siss   Are you going to say it now?

Unn *draws breath, then:*

Unn   No.

Siss *is confused.*

Siss   I'd like to go now.

Unn   Siss?

Siss   Yes.

Unn   It's something serious – I'm not sure I'll go to heaven.

Siss *is shocked, scared. She's got to get out . . .*

Siss   What?

Unn   You heard.

Siss   I have to go now.

Unn   Not yet . . .

Siss   I have to be back before my parents go to bed.

Unn   They won't go to bed yet . . .

Siss *stands up.* **Unn** *bars her way.*

Siss   I have to go.

Unn   Why?

Siss   I told you. Let me go.

---

[1] The signal could be as complicated or as simple as you want to make it. The most important thing is that the two girls consider it grave and binding.

Beat.

Unn *unlocks the door without a word.* **Siss** *goes through, starts pulling on her boots and coat.* **Auntie** *appears.*

Auntie   Are you leaving us so soon, Siss?

Siss   Yes.

Auntie   No secrets left?

The girls look at one another.

Siss   Not this evening.

Auntie   Is anything the matter?

Unn   Of course not.

Auntie   Won't you stay and have something to eat?

Unn   She has to go home.

Siss   Yes – thank you for having me.

Auntie   Will you be alright going home?

Siss   I'll be fine.

Auntie   You must run all the way. It's getting colder and colder. Pitch dark too.

Siss   Yes, I will.

Siss *moves to the doorway, but* **Unn** *is already there, facing her.*

Auntie   Unn. . . ? You'll be seeing each other at school tomorrow . . .

Unn *moves away.*

Unn   Of course.

Siss   Yes.

Unn *looks at* **Auntie**. **Auntie** *leaves the two girls alone.*

Siss   Unn. . . ?

Unn   Yes?

It's hard to know what to say now.

Siss   Tomorrow.

Siss *slips out of the house, leaving* **Unn** *in the lighted doorway.* **Siss** *starts to run towards the forest, but stops, turns, raises her hand in the secret promise sign which* **Unn** *gratefully returns.*
Then, into the forest.
As **Siss** *runs among the trunks, the light on* **Unn** *fades and hands slip out of the darkness snatching at her feet and legs.*

Shadows   Run, Sissy, run Sissy, run, run, run!!!

Siss *emerges suddenly into a lighted area where* **Mother** *and* **Father** *stand, surprised to see the state she's in.*

Mother   What on earth, Siss?

Siss   Didn't you. . . ?

Father   What?

Siss *looks behind her. Nothing there.*

Mother   What's wrong?

Siss   Nothing – I was just running.

Mother   How hot you are, as if you've been running for your life!

Siss   I had to come home before you went to bed, that's all.

Father   You knew we wouldn't be in bed for a long time yet . . .

Mother   Now, now, it doesn't matter. What was it like at Unn's?

Siss   It was nice.

Father   I'd never have thought so!

Siss   Why do you say that?

Father   Your long face.

Siss   Why are you picking on me tonight?

Father   Siss. We were just joking!

Siss   Well it's not funny.

Mother   Have we said anything?

Father   No.

Siss *pulls off her boots.*

Mother   Go and have a wash, Siss, it'll make you feel better.

Siss *picks up her boots.*

And I'll finish supper.

Siss   I've already eaten.

Mother   At Unn's?

Siss *nods, leaves the room.*

I hope you still have an appetite.

Father *folds up his newspaper.*

Father   Loss of appetite is strictly for the young.

The parents move off.

In her bedroom, **Siss** *has taken off her shirt. She sits in her vest before a bowl of water, fastens her hair out of her face, looks down into the bowl, still breathing hard. The light comes up again on* **Unn** *gazing out.* **Siss** *stares down into the water.*

Unn   And we're the same height too.

To the water.

Siss   Yes. Yes. Yes.

Siss *splashes the water over her face happily as* **Unn**'s *light fades and* **Siss**'s *comes down to:*

Blackout.

Scene Two

Unn's house and Siss's house.

The ice cracks and the lights come up on the two homes.
Both Siss *and* Unn *pull on their coats and pick up schoolbags.*

Auntie You're early this morning.

Unn Really?

Auntie I'd say so.

Unn I want to meet Siss.

Auntie I thought as much. Unn – slow down!

Unn What?

Auntie You fasten your coat well first – it's bitter out.

Unn Okay, okay.

Auntie And you take an extra pair of mittens.

Unn *takes them from her.*

Now.

Auntie *opens her arms, they embrace.*

Siss *dashes out of her house.* **Mother** *appears in the doorway, calls.*

Mother I can't see why you have to go so early . . .

Siss Usually you complain I'm so late!

Mother Take care!

Siss *heads into the forest.*
Unn *breaks away from* **Auntie**, *heads into the forest. They walk in determined circles through the trees, crossing one another's paths but oblivious to the fact.*
The ice cracks again. They stop dead. **Siss** *shouts loud in reply.*

Siss I am going to meet Unn!

Unn I am going to meet Siss!

Then they begin hurrying along again. The sound of birds suddenly leaving the trees. The two girls stop, look up. Then:

Siss But what if she's embarrassed after last night?

Unn But what if she's frightened after last night?

They scurry along again, stopping only when they speak.

Unn I can't meet her today. Only think about her.

Siss But surely it won't matter . . .

Unn I won't think of anything bad today, not at all. Only think of Siss, now that I've found her.

Siss After all, we are friends now.

Unn But what should I do all day if not go to school. . . ?

They resume walking again, until **Siss** *rushes round a corner and comes face to face with another running child. The two frighten one another –* **Siss** *is particularly startled, cries out. But it's only* **Inge**.

Inge Sorry!

Siss It's okay, I thought you were . . .

Inge Who?

Siss *stops herself.*

Siss I can't say.

Inge The bogeyman!

Siss (*lying*) Yes!

Inge I knew it!

Siss Are you always so early?

Inge I'm running an errand for my mum before school. How about you?

Siss Couldn't sleep!

Inge Hey, d'you want to go skating after school? There's a few of us getting together . . .

Siss Maybe . . .

Inge The ice was never better!

Siss Have you been to the frozen waterfall yet?

Unn The ice palace!

Inge The ice palace? No.

Siss My father says it's more than ten years since it last froze up. I was a baby then – we all were!

Unn That's where I'll go!

Inge Everyone's talking about it.

Unn But I wanted to see it with Siss . . .

Siss Maybe we'll go at the weekend!

Inge Brilliant! I have to run, now. D'you want to run with me?

Siss No, it's okay. See you later.

Inge Bye!

Inge *races off through the woods, disappears.* **Unn***'s head appears round a tree.* **Siss** *resumes walking.*

Unn   I'll see it the second time with Siss – even better!

Siss *stops, looks round.* **Unn** *hides again.*

Siss   Do you ever get the feeling. . . ?

Siss *sees nothing, hurries on.* **Unn** *watches her until she is out of sight. Whispers:*

Unn   See you tomorrow, Siss. Tomorrow will be the real beginning of everything.

Unn *disappears back into the forest.*

Scene Three

Siss *arrives at school. The* **Teacher** *is just setting out the chairs.*

Teacher   Siss. Isn't this a little early for you?

Siss   I'm turning over a new leaf.

Teacher   We'll see if you can manage it again tomorrow before we jump to any conclusions. Would you finish this?

Siss   Of course.

The **Teacher** *leaves* **Siss** *setting out the chairs in rows. When she has finished, she sits in her own chair, near the front and closes her eyes. Enjoys the sensation of imagining what's behind her.*

Do you ever get the feeling you're being watched?

She flicks her head round suddenly, but of course, there's nobody there.

Overhead, on the banks of the river, **Unn** *walks by, her arms outstretched like wings, balancing as she goes.*

A schoolbell rings offstage. The **Teacher** *walks in swinging it in his/her hand. The children enter in talkative gaggles.* **Siss** *waits by the door.*

Torill   What's up, Siss?

Siss   Why?

Torill   I don't know – you seem . . .

Siss   I'm fine.

All the seats except **Unn**'s *and* **Siss**'s *are filled.* **Siss** *looks out of the door.*

Teacher   Siss?

She looks round.

Let's not spoil that new leaf.

Siss   Oh – no.

Reluctantly, **Siss** *takes her place*

Teacher   Unn is missing today, I see. Does anyone know why?

Some of the class look at **Siss**.

Teacher   No. Oh well. Now, who has not finished their assignment?

The class looks round. No one.

Good. A volunteer to read?

No one volunteers.

Siss, perhaps, to consolidate her promising start to the day?

Siss *grimaces. Stands.*

Which of our opening phrases did you choose?

Siss *starts to read out her story.*

Siss   'The ice on the lake shone bright as polished steel.'

Unn *appears overhead again. Looks out over the 'lake'. The sound of the river faint in the background.*

Siss *looks to the* **Teacher** *for approval. She nods.*

Teacher   Good. A simile. What's a simile?

Torill   When we say a thing is like another thing.

Teacher   Yes. So what's a metaphor? Siss?

Siss   When we say it is the other thing.

Teacher   Very good.

She nods for **Siss** *to continue. As she speaks,* **Unn** *inspects the ice at the edge of the lake.*

Siss   'Inside the ice were leaves, reeds, seeds and twigs from the trees. A brown ant was trapped among the bubbles which looked like beads when the sun caught them.'

Unn *lies down, slides forward a little way onto the ice. Peers through it.*

'The girl lay flat on the ice, not yet feeling the cold. Her body was a shadow for a stranger one down below. She slid forward over the ice –

Unn *does so.*

– to the place where the lake falls away and you must be careful if you're not a good swimmer. The shadow followed her, fell down into the lake and disappeared. The girl was scared. But then she saw it again. It looked as if she were lying down below in the clear water. She felt dizzy. How lucky she was lying safe on top of thick thick ice!'

Unn *pulls back from the ice. Gets up and moves away.*

Teacher   Very good, Siss. Thank you.

Siss *sits down.*

Teacher   And what do we think the girl might do next?

Hands shoot up.
Unn *appears on the lower level, runs through the schoolroom, weaving in and out of her classmates, following the course of the river.*

Teacher Yes.

S/he points to a boy.

Erik She might fetch her skates and go out on the ice.

Teacher Good. Yes. She might.

The **Teacher** *points to a girl whose hand is up.*
Unn *starts to climb back up to the higher level, still following the river, but there's a new sound now, a roaring in the distance, getting louder as she approaches the top.*

Torill She might go home and have some hot chocolate.

Teacher Yes.

S/he points to another girl.

Helle She might go and skim stones in the river.

Teacher Good.

Points to another.

Klaus She might follow the river down to the frozen waterfall.

Teacher And then?

Klaus She might know it was a special place because it only comes in the coldest winters, and it vanishes again in the Spring.

Unn *has reached the top.*

Teacher Good! See how so many different stories can follow from this simple beginning?

The students address themselves to their work.
The roaring of the water becomes deafening. **Unn** *puts her hands over her ears, looks down over the partly frozen fall.*

As **Unn** *gets closer to the edge the 'fall' shines blue and green below, puffs of mist rise into the air.* **Unn** *is ecstatic, shouts for joy.*

Unn Hallo!

But the sound is lost. She tries to get closer to the fall, finds a place to climb down and squeeze inside. Inside is dark and spooky. She calls out.

Unn Hey!

An Echo answers.

Echo Hey!

Unn *is surprised, scared. Tentatively investigates, moving towards the* **Echo**, *squeezing between columns of ice into another area.*

Unn   Hey. . . ?

Echo   Hey. . . ?

Unn *presses on into the next room, which seems to be a kind of ice forest. She's intimated by the strangely human structures that form it. Calls out:*

Unn   Hey. . . ?

She waits for the reply. There's no answer. **Unn** *senses danger, starts to panic, looks for a way out. Then the* **Echo** *calls:*

Echo   Hey!

Unn *calls back, relieved.*

Unn   Hey

Unn *finds that she is at a doorway, squeezes through into another room, distinguished by a constant dripping sound. A drop of water lands on the back of* **Unn**'s *neck, then her nose, then onto her outstretched hands. But the dripping sound is slowly overtaken by another. Someone is crying.*

As the sound of the crying increases, **Unn** *finds that she too is crying. Then the other crying stops and* **Unn**'s *cries echo alone. She is afraid again, tries to find a way out – tries to wriggle through a gap, but it's too narrow.*

She takes off her satchel and coat and tries again – this time she slips through into a bright watery green room. A much happier place, filled with the roaring of the water.

Unn *looks around, calls out.*

Unn   Hallo!

A string of **Echoes** *from different directions calls back.*

Echo   Hallo! Hallo! Hallo!

Unn   Hallo Siss!

Echo   Hallo Siss! Hallo Siss! Hallo Siss!

In the classroom below **Siss** *looks round to* **Unn**'s *desk, disturbed by something.*

Unn   Mother!

Echo   Mother! Mother! Mother!

Unn   Siss!

Echo   Siss! Siss! Siss!

Unn is happier now, finds a dry place and sits down. Rubs her arms against the cold.
The Teacher taps on the top of the desk.

Teacher   Siss?

Siss *faces front.*

Are you listening?

Siss   Sorry.

Siss *goes back to her work.*
The Teacher looks up and down the class.

Teacher   Isn't there anybody who's friends with Unn and knows if she might be ill?

The class look round at one another, at Siss.
Beat.

Is she so lonely?

Siss   No, she's not.

Teacher   Siss?

Siss   Yes.

Teacher   Do you know what's wrong with Unn today?

Siss   I haven't seen her today.

Teacher   But you are her friend?

Siss   Yes.

Helle   No she's not!

Siss   What do you know?

Teacher   There's no need for that!

Siss   I was with Unn at her house last night.

Teacher   And she was alright then?

Siss   Yes, she was.

Teacher   Good. Well in that case perhaps you'd call in on the way home and find out what's the matter. You don't mind the extra walk, do you?

Siss   No.

Teacher   Thank you. So now we've established that, perhaps you could all continue with your work.

The children put their heads down again, but all secretly watch Siss after her outburst.
The Teacher watches her too. Siss is aware of it too, keeps her face close to her book.

In the ice palace, **Unn** *sits sleepily. Then a red glow seems to penetrate the ice, burn towards her. As the red light of the winter sun starts to fill the palace, the sound of the dripping water starts to play a strange insistent tune, a child's lullaby.*

Unn   Did you ever get the feeling . . .

The red beam gets stronger. Shines hard into **Unn***'s face. She stares hard back.*

. . . you were being watched?

She becomes transfixed, at first as though she's afraid of the light, but then as though it's someone she recognises . . . someone she's been waiting for . . . She smiles.

What are you looking for? Here I am. I've been here all the time.

Unn *laughs to herself, delighted.*
Siss *looks up at all the faces around her.*

Unn   I'm not afraid. I haven't done anything . . .

Unn *stretches out her arms in the warmth.*

You won't go away will you. . . ? No. No, not this time.

Unn *curls towards the wall, and goes to sleep.*
In the classroom.

Teacher   Now before you leave . . . the weather report indicates a change this afternoon. It seems the cold spell is coming to an end and the lake will no longer be safe for skating.

Groans of disappointment

On the other hand, it also means that there is an increased possibility of . . .

A ripple of excitement runs around the class.

Helle   Is it. . . ?

Erik   Will it?

Teacher   Snow.

Klaus *is already out of his seat and out of the door. As the others hurriedly pack up.*

Torill   Shall I walk with you to Unn's house, Siss?

Siss   There's no need.

Torill   Suit yourself.

Klaus *rushes back in, plunges his hand into his satchel and pulls out a handful of 'snow'. Tosses it over his head.*

Erik   It's started!

The others follow suit, cheering. As the snow is thrown, we are out of the classroom and on the way home. As **Siss** *fights her way through the crowd of schoolmates they toss the* *'snow' over her. She keeps struggling to the front of the over-excited group, then getting pushed to the back.*

Finally she breaks away and gets ahead of them in the forest. **Siss** *runs now, runs and runs until she emerges near* **Unn**'s. *There is a covering of snow over everything.*

Auntie *carries a pile of wood back towards the house.* **Siss** *sees her, calls.*

Siss Auntie?

Auntie *looks round, is surprised.*

Auntie Oh it's you, Siss. (*Then.*) Has something happened to Unn?

Siss What?

Auntie Why have you come and not Unn?

Siss But surely, Unn's at home. . . ?

Auntie Didn't she come to school this morning?

Siss *shakes her head, suddenly starts to feel afraid.*

Oh no . . . oh no . . .

Auntie *runs around to the side of the house.* **Siss** *follows a little way, but* **Auntie** *reappears and runs to the other side.*

Siss Where is she?

Auntie Run home, Siss, run home and raise the alarm, quick before it gets dark. Run home and raise the alarm. Go!

Auntie *hurries off in the opposite direction. After a moment,* **Siss** *dashes back into the forest, her* **Father** *appears almost immediately, catches her in his arms, lifts her up.* **Siss** *cries out.*

Siss Unn has gone! She's disappeared!

As **Siss** *turns high in the air, the forest starts to fill with orange lanterns, swinging in the darkness as the search begins.*

Scene Four

The Forest.

The low tones of the adults calling out:

Searchers Unn!

The search party swarms about, converging and dispersing.

Searcher 1 If only the snow had come yesterday!

Searcher 2 Then there would have been tracks.

Searcher 1 Now it's come too late and made matters worse.

Searcher 3 After this we'll search up near the lake.

Searcher 2 What would she be doing up there?

Searcher 4 What would she be doing anywhere?

Searcher 1 Sh!!! Quiet now!

They stop suddenly, listen hard. Nothing.

Searcher 1 Sorry. I thought . . .

Searcher 3 Just a bird.

Searcher 2 Let's keep moving.

In the darkness, **Siss***'s voice calls out too as her* **Father** *drags her towards home.*

Siss Unn! Unn!

Father Siss, listen to me . . . we can't have you running about in the night and the storm.

Siss I'm going. I have to . . .

Mother *arrives.*

Father There are other ways of helping, Siss.

Siss No . . .

Father Sh, quiet down now and tell me: what happened when you were with Unn last night? Was there anything special?

Siss *hesitates.*

Siss No.

Father Are you sure?

Mother Did she say anything?

Siss No.

Mother   You were upset when you got home, Siss.

Siss   I can't tell you.

Father   For God's sake, Siss if you know anything about this . . .

Siss   I don't! But I must come with you . . .

Father   No.

Siss   Yes!

Mother   Maybe she should . . . I mean look how upset she is . . . We don't know what this is all about. Perhaps she can help . . .

Siss   Father, please!

Father   Okay, only stay close by. No wandering off, understood?

Siss   Yes.

Mother   We mean it.

Siss *and her* **Father** *head off and join up with the other searchers.*

Father   Any luck?

Searcher 1   Not so far, but we'll search all night if we have to.

Searcher 2   She'll never survive out of doors.

Searcher 1   I can't help thinking of the road . . . the cars driven by all sorts of people.

Father   Strangers.

Searcher 1   Exactly. It's Siss, isn't it?

Father   That's right.

Searcher 1   Inge said you were with Unn last night?

Siss   I don't know anything. I'm going to look down the hill.

Father   Don't lose sight of us for a second.

Siss   I won't . . .

Siss *makes her way through the trees to lower down the hill. Crouches down. Looks out, scanning the night with quiet determination.*

One of the searchers makes their way to **Auntie**'s. *She waits outside the front door with* **Siss**'s **Mother**, *exhausted, impassive.*

Searcher 5   Anything?

Auntie *shakes her head.*

Mother   We've been telephoning all over, but there's no news.

Searcher 5   Well . . . no news is good news, I suppose.

Auntie *seems unconvinced.*

We had another idea.

Auntie *nods.*

Searcher 5   What about the frozen waterfall?

Auntie   The ice palace?

Searcher 5   There's supposed to have been some talk of a school trip to it. The young ones've never seen it before. Could Unn have gone there on her own and got lost?

Auntie   To play truant from school, it's not like her.

Searcher 5   What would be like her then?

Auntie   I don't know. She is simply like herself.

Searcher 5   Has she any friends?

Auntie   Yesterday one of the girls from school was here – for the first time since Unn came to live with me.

Searcher 5   Who was that?

Mother   My daughter, Siss.

Auntie   But she can't tell you anything. She's as shocked as anyone about all this.

Mother   There was something she didn't want to say.

Searcher 5   What?

Auntie   Something they were giggling about I expect. Siss is a good girl, and she is Unn's friend. She would help us if she could.

Searcher 5   Why did the snow have to come now?

Mother   It's always the way.

Auntie *turns away from them and heads inside.* **Mother** *and* **Searcher 5** *whisper to one another so that* **Auntie** *can't hear.*
On the hillside, **Siss** *repeats over and over:*

Siss   Nothing must happen to Unn, nothing must happen to Unn, nothing must happen to Unn, nothing must happen to . . .

An exuberant cry comes out of nowhere.

Mats   She's here – she's here! I see her!

An older boy, **Mats**, *scrambles down the hill towards* **Siss**. *She jumps up, looking for* **Unn**, *but he grabs her.*

Oh no you don't!

His arms are around her.

I knew I'd find you! I knew you'd be alright.

Siss   But it's not me!

Mats   Of course it's you.

Siss   No, I'm looking for Unn too.

Mats   You're not Unn?

Siss   No. I'm Siss.

He pushes her away from him, despondent.

Mats   What are you playing at down here?

Siss   I'm looking.

The other searchers appear. He calls out to them.

Mats   It's not her – it's the other one. I'm sorry . . .

The searchers shake their heads, move away.

(*To* **Siss**.) You should be at home.

Siss   I'm the only one who knows her.

He walks away to rejoin the others. **Siss** *shouts after him.*

And I'm staying till she's found!

A **Man** *breaks away from the group*

Searcher 2   Come over here, Siss.

Siss   I'm busy searching.

Searcher 2   Just come here.

The **Man** *grabs* **Siss** *by the arm.*

I'm surprised you're allowed out so late.

The others approach.

Siss   It's none of your business.

Searcher 2   You said you know something about Unn.

Searcher 3   You were with her yesterday evening . . .

Searcher 2   What did you talk about?

Searcher 3   Was there anything she told you?

Searcher 4   She said something, didn't she?

Searcher 2   You must tell us.

Searcher 3   It might save Unn's life!

Siss   She didn't say anything about this.

Searcher 2   What do you mean?

Siss   About going anywhere.

Searcher 3   Was it something that could help us look for her?

Siss   No.

Searcher 4   What did Unn tell you?

Siss   Nothing.

Searcher 2   We can see you know something. Now, what did Unn say?

Siss   I can't tell you.

Searcher 2   Why not?

Siss   It wasn't like that.

Searcher 3   Siss . . .

Siss *shouts out.*

Siss   No, I can't stand it!

The searchers are shocked. They back off a little.

Searcher 2   She's exhausted.

Searcher 3   We're wasting our time.

The men start to move away.

Searcher 4   It's a shame you won't tell us. You might have helped find her.

They all move off back into the woods, their lanterns still visible among the trees.
Searcher 1 *arrives, preoccupied.*

Searcher 1   Ah, Siss. Did Unn want to go and see the big pile of ice. . . ?

Siss   I don't know.

Searcher 1   Weren't there plans for the whole school to go?

Siss   I suppose . . .

Searcher 1   Could she have gone by herself? After all, she'd no friends.

Siss   That's not true! She had me!

Siss *becomes hysterical, hits out at* **Searcher 1**.

She had me, she had me . . .

Searcher 1 *tries to hold* **Siss** *still.* **Siss** *struggles, calls out.*

Siss   Father! Father!

A voice out of the night.

Father   (*offstage*) Siss?

Father *starts towards them.*

Father   What's this?

Searcher 1 *releases* **Siss** *and she rushes to her* **Father**.

Siss   She had me.

Searcher 1   She's soaked through . . . exhausted . . .

Father   I'm taking you home.

Siss   But you promised.

Father   I thought it would be over by now.

Siss   I'm just as good a walker as any of them.

Searcher 1   We're following the river to the waterfall. Unn may have taken it into her head to go there and then got lost.

Searcher 1 *sets off without them.*

Siss   Father, please!

Father   Okay, okay. But keep close by, I don't want to have to keep looking for you when I should be looking for Unn.

Siss *holds out her hand.* **Father** *takes it and she leads him after* **Searcher 1** *into the night.*
Ahead of them, a search party thrashes at the riverbank with sticks. In the distance, voices cry out **Unn**'s *name.*

Searcher 2   How can you see anything with the river like a mirror?

Searcher 3   Anything could be hidden and sucked away down there.

Searcher 4   Don't think about it.

Searcher 3   No, you're right.

Searcher 2   Still, it doesn't look good.

Searcher 4   We're falling behind. Look at the lanterns on the other side. They're much further ahead. They'll be at the ice fall before us.

They pick up speed, still searching in the undergrowth.
Up above, **Searcher 1** *appears, tailed by* **Siss** *and her* **Father**. **Siss** *is calling out,*

combing the land with her tired eyes. The sound of the waterfall comes up – they have reached it. **Siss** *is amazed by it, overwhelmed.*

Searcher 1   I'll try and cut down, get a better look.

S/he struggles further down. Lifts the lantern. The palace flickers. **Siss** *is afraid.*

Bring your lanterns!

They move closer. **Siss***'s* **Father** *calls to the rest of the search party.*

Father   Bring your lights!

As the lanterns mass, some of the splendour of the ice palace is glimpsed. The crowd stand dumbstruck at the sight of it. After a moment . . .

Searcher 1   I'll see if I can find a way in.

They watch as s/he struggles to negotiate the structure, finding gaps in it which turn out to be dead ends, until:

There's something here . . . a gap I mean.

S/he squeezes in a little further.

No. Someone smaller might do it though . . .

Everyone's attention turns to **Siss***, but* **Father** *pulls her close to him, shakes his head. A voice in the crowd:*

Mats   Shall I try?

He clambers down and tries to force his way in. Gets a bit further but not much.

It's no good. There may have been an opening earlier but it's frozen up now.

The searchers stand helpless, considering the implications of this. In **Siss***'s head, a sound starts to echo . . . the dislocated sound of a girl's laughter . . .*
Searcher 4 *calls to* **Siss***, making her the focus of all eyes.*

Searcher 4   You're sure Unn didn't say anything about coming here?

Siss *is distracted, distant.*

Siss   No . . .

Father   That's enough, now. Siss is not to be questioned any more.

Searcher 1   She's told us what she knows.

Searcher 4   I'm sorry . . . I . . . I meant no harm, it's only . . .

Searcher 2   There are so many chasms she could have fallen into.

Searcher 1   If she came here.

Searcher 3   If.

Siss *watches as the searchers swing their lanterns around the structure. Their sticks strike at it sporadically, then stop. The girl's laughter in her head echoes louder and louder and louder until it is no longer laughter but the sound of someone crying out.*
Siss *cries out too – a terrible long scream. The searchers stop dead still.*

Father   Siss?

She shrieks at them, hysterical.

Siss   Why are you just standing here? As if you'd given up. Unn is not dead! She's not . . .

The searchers look at one another, embarrassed.

We have to find her!

Siss *starts to run away from the Ice Palace.*

Father   I'll catch you up . . .

He races after her. The searchers look on.

Scene Five

Siss*'s bedroom.*

A figure lies under a white sheet on Siss*'s bed.* Siss *runs into the room, pulling off her clothes, throwing her coat and sweater onto the floor. She kicks her trousers off.* Siss *finally notices the bed, stops. The figure sits up in bed, peeps over the sheet.*

Unn Hallo Siss.

Siss *is astonished, overjoyed.*

Siss Unn? Is it you?

Unn Well who else would I be if not myself?

Siss I'm not myself at the moment.

Unn Oh. Who are you instead?

Siss I don't know.

Unn Are we still friends?

Siss Oh yes. More than ever.

Unn Then you are Siss. Because she is my only friend. Here, you're the one supposed to be in bed.

Unn *gets out of the bed.*

Siss Am I?

Unn Oh yes! Doctor's orders!

They laugh. **Siss** *gets into the bed.*

Now I'll take care of you.

Siss Unn?

Unn Yes.

Siss I didn't tell anyone.

Unn Tell them what?

Siss Anything.

Unn But what was there to tell?

Mother *comes in, smiling.*

Mother Siss!

Siss Isn't it wonderful?

Mother   I know, I thought I was lost forever!

Siss *is baffled.*

Siss   You?

Mother   What is it, Siss?

Unn   What is it, Siss?

Mother   Lie down again.

Unn   Here, lie down again.

Siss   (*to* **Mother**) But can't you see Unn?

Mother   Only if I look in the mirror!

Mother *looks at* **Unn**. *They both laugh. They talk while they straighten* **Siss**'s *bed, with her in it. Dialogue is now split between* **Mother** *and* **Unn**.

Mother   You're not

Unn   well

Mother   Siss

Unn   you

Mother   have a

Unn   high

Mother   fever.

Siss *looks from one to the other.*

Mother   It was too

Unn   much for you

Mother   out in the

Unn   woods last

Mother   night.

Unn   You

Mother   came home

Unn   ill.

Siss   But Unn . . .

Mother ⎫
Unn ⎬   Unn hasn't been found.

Siss *can't bear the confusion any longer.*

Siss   She was here. Just now.

Mother   No, Siss. You're dreaming.

Unn   Feel how hot you are.

Siss   No, I'm cold. I'm freezing cold.

Siss *is distressed.*

Mother   Sh . . .

Mother *hugs her.*

It's alright, Siss.

Siss   I was out with the men.

Mother   It was too much for you . . .

Siss   We were at the big pile of ice.

Unn   Your father brought you back.

Mother   You managed to walk, I don't know how. The doctor says . . .

Siss   What time is it?

Mother   It's evening now.

Siss   Where's father?

Mother   Out with the search party still.

Siss   They *are* still searching?

Unn   Of course.

Siss   It was so like Unn in here earlier. She can't be far away.

Mother   I hope not.

Unn   I'm sure.

Siss *looks at them both.*

Siss   I need to sleep now.

Siss *pulls the covers over her head.*

Go away now. Go out of the room.

Mother *and* **Unn** *hesitate.*

Go on . . .

They give in and leave **Siss** *alone. Slowly and silently the room fills with her schoolmates. They whisper.*

All   Siss . . . Siss . . . Siss . . . Siss . . . Siss . . . Siss . . . Siss . . . Siss . . .

Siss *stays buried under the covers.*

Siss   I need to sleep now.

They gather up the sheet and **Siss** *inside it, swing it between them, singing.*

All   Rockabye baby on the tree top . . .

Siss *struggles against them.*

Siss   No . . . Put me down.

All   Secret, secret, who's got a secret?

Unn *enters.*
The crowd pull the sheet taut and start to give **Siss** *the 'bumps'.*

Unn   Tom tale tit! Your tongue will split, and all the little birdies will have a little bit!!

Siss   I'll never tell.

Unn   Remember your promise!

Siss   I do . . .

Unn   Goodbye.

Unn *waves goodbye and starts to walk away.* **Siss** *calls after her.*

Siss   But where. . . ? When. . . ? Unn don't go away . . . I've only just found you . . .

But the bouncing continues and she can't follow.

Unn!!!

All   And one for luck!

There's a high bounce and then the sheet is lowered back onto the bed, **Siss** *covered over with it, before the schoolchildren melt away.* **Siss** *lies under the sheet. Her* **Mother** *comes in. Touches her through the sheet.* **Siss** *sits upright suddenly, woken from a deep sleep. Looks around her.*

Mother   Feeling any better?

Siss *eyes her with suspicion, tries to get her bearings.*

You've had a good rest.

Siss   Has anyone been in here?
Father came in just now. He wanted to ask you about something, but you were asleep.

She feels **Siss**'*s forehead – cooler now.* **Siss** *collects herself a little.* **Mother** *continues.*

He said it was important.

Siss   Is there news?

Mother   No.

Siss   Oh.

Mother   Siss . . . you must try and remember what you and Unn really did talk about . . .

Siss   Oh, no!

Mother   . . . what she said to you. That's what Father has to know . . . if only you can give them some hint.

Siss   I told you it was nothing.

Mother   But are you sure, Siss?

Siss   Of course.

Mother   While you were feverish you talked about the strangest things.

Siss *starts to panic.*

Siss   What did I say?

Mother   It's better for you to tell us.

Siss   I can't.

Mother   Tell us, Siss . . . This is all for Unn's sake . . .

Siss   But when I say I can't tell you I can't do any more, can I?

Mother   Just tell us!

Suddenly **Siss** *is furious.*

Siss   She didn't say it, I tell you! She didn't tell me anything, why don't you believe me, why doesn't anyone believe me?

Siss *collapses into hysterical tears.*

I am Unn's friend . . . I don't want my tongue to split . . .

Mother *is shocked.*

Mother   Siss, Siss it's alright.

Siss   No it's not . . . it never will be . . .

Mother   Siss, I didn't know . . . I didn't know . . .

Siss   Nothing will ever be right again . . .

Mother *rocks the sobbing* **Siss** *in her arms.*

Nothing will ever be right . . .

Scene Six

Auntie's house/**Siss**'s House.

*Outside **Auntie**'s house, a **Man** sweeps a path free of snow. **Auntie** watches.*

Auntie   You're kind.

Man   It's the least I can do.

Auntie   All the same.

*The **Man** nods, continues. After a while.*

Man   I drove into town this morning.

Auntie   Yes?

Man   The picture of her is everywhere. In all the shops. Everyone's talking about it.

Auntie   What're they saying?

Man   Well, there's no news, of course.

Auntie   Of course.

Man   Or you'd have heard.

Auntie *nods.*

I asked around for an hour or so, but . . .

Auntie   I see.

Man   Nothing.

Auntie   Thank you. It can't be helped.

Beat.

Man   She isn't forgotten.

Auntie   No.

Auntie *looks out, ending the conversation. The **Man** goes back to clearing the path.*

Siss *appears in her dressing gown. She looks out towards **Auntie**'s house, stretches out her arms.*

Siss   I promise to think about no one but you. To think about everything I know about you. To think about you at home and at school, and on the way to school. To think about you all day long, and if I wake up at night. I promise.

Siss *makes the secret promise signal.*

Outside **Auntie***'s, two searchers approach carrying tall poles. They dig them into the snow with the others.*

Man   You've been dragging the river?

They nod.

Searcher 1   I don't know what hope there is.

Searcher 2   There comes a time when even bad news would be welcome.

Auntie *approaches.*

Searcher 1   Nothing to tell, I'm afraid.

Auntie   I see. Oh well.

Searcher 1   I didn't know Unn myself.

Auntie   No?

Beat.

I was very fond of her.

The searchers make their way off again.

Man   I'm more or less finished now.

Auntie *nods. The* **Man** *shuffles uncomfortably away.
At* **Siss***'s,* **Siss** *is in bed. She examines her palms.*

Siss   I feel you are so close I could touch you, but I daren't. I feel you looking at me when I lie here in the dark. I remember it all and I promise only to think about that, at school tomorrow. I shall do so every day, as long as you are gone. There is no one else.

At **Auntie***'s, a* **Woman** *approaches.*

Woman   I thought you might want this.

Auntie *takes it. A picture.*

We made it bigger.

Auntie   I heard they were all round town.

Woman   It's a good likeness.

Auntie   Taken last summer.

Woman   She looks so enquiring, don't you think?

Auntie   She lost her mother in the spring. Everything she had. So she had something to enquire about, don't you think?

Woman   Of course. I'm sorry. Yes. Well I should probably . . .

Auntie   Yes.

The **Woman** *leaves.*
Siss *pulls on her clothes. Stops halfway.*

Siss   I feel you standing in the passage, waiting for me when I go out. What are you thinking about? There's still no one but you. No one else. You must believe me when I tell you so, Unn. I shall never forget my promise as long as you are gone.

Siss *makes the promise sign.*
She walks over to **Auntie***'s.*
Auntie *has her back to* **Siss***.*

Siss   Hallo?

Auntie *stiffens. Turns slowly to face* **Siss***. She's obviously happy but also disappointed to see* **Siss***.*

Auntie   Oh, it's you, Siss.

Siss   I'm sorry.

Auntie   Not at all, not at all. No, no. How nice of you to come. Are you well again? I heard you were ill after that trip to the river.

Siss *nods.*

Siss   I'm to go back to school tomorrow.

Auntie   I knew that was why you didn't come. Because you couldn't. Perhaps you'd like to ask me about Unn?

Siss *is a little surprised.*

You must ask if you want to.

Siss   Ask what?

Auntie   Whatever it is you most want to.

Siss *thinks.*

Siss   Nothing.

Auntie   Is it so locked inside you?

Siss *shrugs, looks away. Beat.*

Siss   Are they going to find her?

Auntie   I hope they will every day.

Siss   Can I look in her room?

Auntie   Of course.

Siss *looks.*

Do you want to go in?

Siss *shakes her head.*

Siss   Why is Unn the way she is?

Auntie   Is Unn not as she should be then?

Siss   Unn's nice.

Auntie   And wasn't she happy too, the other evening!

Siss   She wasn't only happy.

Auntie   She can't be only happy when her mother died so recently.

Siss   There was something else as well.

Auntie   What?

Siss   I don't know what. She didn't tell me.

Auntie   They've been here asking and asking till I'm worn out. I know they've been asking you too. You understand they had to?

Siss   I suppose . . .

Auntie   You must forgive my asking too – but I am Unn's aunt – and I think there is a difference. You see, I know nothing about Unn, except what everyone else knows and has seen. Before this, she was all mine – an unexpected windfall if you like, all for me. But now she belongs to everyone it seems. She didn't tell me anything.

Beat.

Did she say something special to you that evening?

Beat.

Siss   No.

Beat.

Auntie   No, of course not. It's not likely Unn would have told you all her secrets the first time you met.

Siss   Can I ask you something?

Auntie   Of course.

Siss   What will happen if she doesn't come back?

Beat.

Auntie   I would not let anyone else ask that, Siss. Though I have thought about it, of course.

Auntie *braces herself.*

If Unn doesn't come back, I shall sell this house and go away. I don't think I can stay here without her. Even though I had her such a short time.

Auntie *hides her tears.*

Well, well, well. We shan't talk about that. Just because Unn hasn't come back yet doesn't mean she won't come back ever.

Siss   No.

Auntie   And nothing will be changed here, don't worry.

Siss   I understand.

Auntie   Everything will be just the same.

Auntie *and* **Siss** *exchange smiles. A moment of shared hope.*

Siss   Yes. Everything exactly as it was.

But their hope is against the odds and they both feel it.

Scene Seven

*School. The class is assembled. There are two empty places: one belonging to **Siss**, the other to **Unn**. The class works in silence, the **Teacher** is at his/her desk. **Siss** enters and a ripple of excitement runs around the room.*

Teacher   All right again, Siss?

Siss   Thank you.

Teacher   That's good.

Siss *sits in her old place.*

I'll fetch you a copy of the new book we've started.

To the class.

And please remember, no gossiping while I am out of the room.

*The moment s/he's gone, the class erupts with excitement, swarming around **Siss**.*

Students   Here you are!
Welcome back!
Are you better?
Was it awful that night?
You don't look sick . . .
And just think, they can't find a trace of Unn.
It's terrible.
Shh!!!
You wouldn't believe it.

Siss *answers 'yes' and 'no'.*

Torill   We went out searching too!

Siss   I know.

Klaus   Now you're back things will be more like before.

Siss   I don't think so.

Erik   Leave her alone!

Inge   What was it? They say Unn told you something you wouldn't . . .

Siss   I can't stand it!

*They back away from **Siss**, surprised by the outburst.*

Erik   Now see what you've done!

The **Teacher** *returns and the students scurry back to their places, but it's clear that something has happened.*

Teacher   There's a lot of excitement in the room.

Erik   We're just glad to have Siss back.

The **Teacher***'s not convinced, but doesn't want to make a fuss.*

Teacher   Shall we settle down again now? And please bear in mind what we discussed yesterday . . .

The students return to their work. **Siss** *opens the new book. Looks at it. Turns to look at* **Unn***'s empty desk. Turns back. Seems unable to work. She looks for* **Unn** *again, then settles to her study.*

The **Teacher** *remains oblivious to what follows unless otherwise indicated.*

A note is passed in secret between the students. It reaches **Siss***. She reads it and looks across the desks to a girl. The girl stage-whispers.*

Inge   Will you play with us at break?

Siss   No.

Siss *screws up the note, but almost immediately another arrives. She looks at a boy behind her.*

Klaus   Do you want to go on a ski trip at the weekend?

Siss   No.

Siss *crumples this note, but now there is a flurry of them winging towards her. Each one she opens brings a new invitation, a babble of whispered friendship. When the frenzy is at its peak,* **Siss** *shouts out.*

Siss   No, that's enough! I can't, don't you understand?

The students go back to their work, **Mother** *appears.*

Mother   Siss?

Siss *scoops up the notes from the desk.*

Siss   They're not thinking about Unn at all.

Mother   Who isn't?

Siss   Nobody is. Everyone's forgotten her.

Mother   You haven't.

Siss   Never!

Mother   Listen, Siss. Other people didn't know Unn very well. And they have a lot to think about. Their own lives. You're the one person who can think about Unn all the time.

Siss *brightens.*

Siss   Really?

Mother   If that's what will make you happy.

Siss   Yes. It will. I'm the one.

She happily tears up the friendship notes.

I'm the one.

Mother   It's good to see you smile, Siss.

Siss *tosses the paper into the air. It falls like snow around her. She laughs.*

They say the thaw is coming. The snow has melted off the big ice pile.

Siss   When the warm wind brings the thaw it might bring Unn back too.

Mother   It might.

Siss   I think it will!

Mother   Siss . . .

But **Siss** *interrupts, exuberant.*

Siss   Thank you.

Mother   Whatever for?

Siss   For the best Christmas present ever.

Mother *shakes her head. She taps the* **Teacher** *on the arm and s/he comes to life. They shake hands and move away from the students, chatting, obviously concerned about* **Siss**. *Then the classroom door opens and a wind blows in through the room, disturbing* **Siss**'s *shredded paper.* **Siss** *seems to be the only one to notice – she turns around, hardly daring to look. The wind dies down. A bright light in the doorway: a girl stands waiting to come in.*

Seeing **Siss**, *the whole class turns to stare. After a moment:*

Siss   Who are you?

Selma   I'm Selma. I'm new.

There's no response from the startled class, but the spell is broken as **Selma** *closes the door behind her.*

I don't know where I'm to sit.

The empty desk is suddenly the focus of all attention. The class defers to **Siss**.

Selma   Is this one free?

Siss   No. It's never free.

*The girl looks around the class for some kind of explanation, but they all look away. She waits until the **Teacher** returns, ushering in a more normal – if tense – atmosphere.*

Teacher   This is Selma, she will be joining us for the rest of the year.

*The **Teacher** bites the bullet.*

You'd better take that desk there. It's free now.

*The girl looks at **Siss**. **Siss** stands.*

Siss   It isn't free.

Teacher   The desk ought to be used, Siss. I think that would be the best way.

Siss   No!

Teacher *looks at class. Senses their agreement.*

There are desks out in the corridor that aren't being used.

Erik   Should I go and fetch one?

Teacher   (*to* **Selma**) The desk belonged to a girl who disappeared last autumn. I expect you read about it in the papers.

Selma   Her name was . . . Unn?

Siss   If her place isn't there, she'll never come back.

Teacher   I think that's going too far. None of us should say things like that.

Siss   Why can't the desk stay as it is?

Teacher   I respect the way you feel, Siss, but you mustn't go too far. Wouldn't it be better for someone to sit there for the time being? That would be quite natural. Nothing would be spoilt by that, would it?

Siss   Yes.

Stares at new girl. Feeling of ill-will.

Selma   I would rather not sit there.

Beat.

Teacher   Alright. Fetch another desk.

Erik *goes.*

Teacher   It's not worth spoiling a thing like this.

*The class's attitude to **Selma** shifts immediately. They make her welcome.*

Inge   (*to* **Siss**) D'you see how we're all in this together?

Siss *is suspicious, reluctant.*

Friends, Siss.

Siss *thinks for a moment, shakes her head.*

But you can't stay alone all the time like this.

Siss   I'm not alone. And I don't want you to ask me about it again.

Inge   You can't go on punishing us like this, Siss. We haven't done anything to hurt you.

Siss   It isn't that . . .

Inge   There's a ski trip on Saturday – why don't you come with us?

Siss   No.

Inge   It's the best time for it now that the drifts have all settled . . .

Siss   I can't.

Inge   We could go to the ice palace. They say it's incredible now the snow's melted off it.

Siss *considers.*

Go on, Siss. Just this once.

Siss   Okay but only if we go there. To the ice palace.

Inge   Agreed.

Siss   Agreed.

Inge   It's a good start.

Siss   It's not any kind of start.

The **Teacher** *taps on his/her desk.*

Teacher   Thank you . . .

Siss *turns away to face front.* **Siss**'s *hand shoots up.*

Siss   I'd like to read.

Everyone is surprised.

Teacher   Well . . . if you wish. It's nice to have a volunteer for a change. You know what page we've reached?

Siss *nods, stands, reads. As she reads, one by one each class member rises solemnly from their seat and takes up a position on the way towards the ice palace.*
By the end of the poem, only **Siss** *and the* **Teacher** *remain. The students regard the distant ice palace with reverence, the atmosphere is almost religious.*

Siss   We stand here and the snow falls thicker,
Your sleeve turns white and so does mine
They hand before us like snow-covered
bridges.
But snow-covered bridges are dead.
In here is living warmth.
Your arm is warm under the weight of snow, and
a welcome weight on mine.
It snows and snows
on silent bridges
Bridges that are unknown to all.

Scene Eight

The Ice Palace. The palace appears in all its glory. The others are ahead of **Siss**. *They wait until* **Siss** *joins them, observe the ice palace in awestruck silence. This is their tragedy too.*

After a while.

Inge   Well. Where shall we go next?

Siss   I only wanted to come here.

Helle   Why here?

Torill   Siss must decide. If she doesn't want to come any further it's none of our business.

Siss   I'm turning back now.

Inge   We'll turn back too then.

Siss   Can't you go on as planned?

Erik   But why not come with us?

Siss   I'd like to be alone here for a bit.

The others look at one another, seem to defer silently to **Torill**.

Torill   You don't want to be with us any more today?

Siss   I'd rather not.

Torill *shrugs. What can she do? Faces fall.*

It's something that I've promised.

Helle   We thought everything was going to be the way it was before . . .

Siss   How could it?

Her friends give up. One by one, they begin to disappear. **Siss** *watches for a while, then the roar of the fall draws her back. She shouts over the noise.*

Siss   There's still no one but you. No one else. You must believe me when I tell you so Unn. I shall never forget my promise as long as you are gone.

Siss *makes the promise sign.*
For a moment, **Unn** *appears inside the ice – clearly, distinctly and dead.* **Siss** *backs away, terrified.*
Unn's *disembodied voice echoes through the roar.*

Unn   (v.o) What are you looking for? Here I am. I've been here all the time.

Siss *watches appalled until a cloud moves across the sun and* **Unn** *disappears again. She shouts out for her friend.*

Siss Unn!

She starts to approach the ice, backs off.

What does this mean?

She starts to understand.

Oh no . . .

Siss *thinks for a moment longer.*

Unn is dead.

She shouts at the ice.

Unn is dead!

Siss *runs back down and into the forest, dazed with grief. She emerges near* **Auntie***'s. Stands looking at* **Auntie***'s house.*

Scene Nine

Auntie's. **Auntie** *comes out of her house, calls.*

Auntie Siss? What a coincidence . . .

Siss Why?

Auntie *can see that* **Siss** *is upset.*

Auntie I was hoping to speak to you, that's all.

Siss There's no news of Unn, is there.

Auntie No.

Siss No.

Auntie Would you like to come in?

Siss *shakes her head.*

Are you alright, Siss?

Siss I don't know. I can't say it.

Auntie Well I should say something then . . . I believe I promised to tell you if I were to sell and leave.

Siss *understands.*

Siss Oh.

Auntie I'm certain now that there's nothing more to wait for.

Siss *looks back towards the waterfall – she's certain too.*

Siss Do you *know* that?

Auntie I don't *know* – and yet I do know just the same. So I've sold the cottage, and I'm going away.

Siss When?

Auntie Tomorrow.

The news sinks in. **Siss** *can feel her last real link with* **Unn** *slipping away.* **Auntie** *resumes nervously. In many ways,* **Siss** *is her last link with* **Unn**.

Auntie I was lucky I saw you. Otherwise I was thinking I'd look in on you this evening. My last evening. I'd like to go for a walk. I was hoping you might come with me.

Siss Where do you want to go?

Auntie Just around and about.

Siss   I'll have to call my parents, tell them I'll be late.

Auntie   They won't mind?

Siss   They'll be glad I've found something to do. Have you packed?

Auntie *nods.*

Auntie   Would you like to look in?

Siss *creeps to the window. Looks.*

Siss   Empty.

Auntie   Do you want to go inside?

Siss   No. Yes.

Auntie *nods.* **Siss** *enters. The room where everything took place. Now empty. Finished.* **Siss** *comes out.*

Let's go now, shall we.

Auntie   Just the two of us.

Siss   Yes.

Auntie   This is nobody's business but ours.

They set out. Through the forest, uphill to a vantage point from which they can look down over the village. The lights on the model village gradually come on.

Auntie   Siss, I didn't ask you along just for the company.

Siss   I didn't think so.

Auntie   I may live alone, but I hear things. You've had a difficult winter. Cut yourself off from your friends at school, even from your parents.

Siss   I made a promise.

Auntie   Ah. I knew it must be something of the sort. And I suppose I should be grateful to you – for the sake of kinship, so to speak.

Auntie *brushes* **Siss***'s cheek with her hand, but it's too upsetting a gesture. She pulls away.*

I don't want you to tell me any more about it. But you mustn't promise so much that you destroy yourself. Especially when there's no point in it any more.

Siss   You don't understand . . .

Auntie   You've been ill!

Siss   I couldn't stand it. They went on and on about something I couldn't tell them . . . over and over.

Auntie   You must remember it was at the very beginning when we had to try everything. None of us realised it was so hard on you.

Siss   They've stopped now.

Auntie   Yes they made sure of that.

Siss   Made sure of it?

Auntie   The doctor who came to see you drummed it into them at school, too. How important it was not to mention it.

Siss   (*surprised*) I didn't know.

Auntie   You were very depressed. There's no reason not to tell you now that it's over.

Siss   Is it over?

Auntie   Yes.

Beat.

I suppose we must talk about that too, mustn't we? You mustn't think people have forgotten who they were searching for. They haven't. I know that. They've given me so much help that now I'm leaving I don't know what to do about it. I ought to have gone round to thank them all. But I can't.

Siss   No.

Auntie   That's why I'm walking out here in the dark this evening. I daren't show my face.

Siss   You must tell me what's over.

Auntie *struggles to find the words.*

Auntie   Alright, Siss . . . Unn is gone, and she's not alive.

Siss   Have you found something out?

Auntie   Not exactly . . . and yet I know it, just the same. What I want to ask you before I leave is that you try to go back to all that you used to have. You said you made a promise. But it can't come to anything now that the other person isn't here any more. You can't bind yourself to a memory, shut yourself away from what is natural to you. Are you listening?

Siss   Yes, yes of course.

Auntie   Alright: she will not come back and you are freed from your promise.

Siss *is taken aback.*

Siss   Can you do that?

Auntie   I believe I can. Right here and now.

Siss   Freed?

Auntie   Shall we say now that it is over? Make an agreement?

Siss   How can I know if it's true? Whether you can do it for me?

Auntie   Has it gone so deep, Siss? You must have wondered how long you could go on . . .

Siss   But it was a promise . . .

Auntie   It will be alright, Siss. Trust me. Just so I can be a little happier about going away.

Something moves in the trees. It's something. It's nothing.

It's not right for you to go on as you are. So unlike yourself.

Siss   No.

Auntie *seems to have made some headway – as much as she can.*

Auntie   So. That is that. We can cut through here to your house, can't we, Siss?

Siss   Couldn't I see you home?

Auntie   There's no need.

Siss   I'm not afraid of the dark. Not any more.

Auntie   Alright.

They walk.

Siss   It's not cold.

Auntie   Not a bit.

Siss   What'll you do in the place where you're going to live?

Auntie   Oh, I shall find something to busy myself with. You mustn't worry about me.

Siss   No.

Auntie   I'm a worthless creature.

Siss   Don't say that . . .

Auntie The people here have done everything they could for me. Now I'm going to leave without saying goodbye. Don't you think that's poor behaviour, Siss?

Siss I don't know . . .

Auntie You are my consolation . . . since you went round with me this evening, they'll find out that I walked the village boundary. And perhaps they'll understand that I did it as a way of thanking them. That's something. I'm counting on your telling them. Though I know only a worthless creature would think that way.

Siss No. No, I'll tell them. I promise.

Siss *makes the promise sign to* **Auntie**. *They are back at* **Auntie**'s *house now.*

Auntie No need to promise, Siss. If you say it, then I know it's true. Well here I am then. Back where I began.

Auntie *seems reluctant to part from* **Siss**.

Let's make an end to it, Siss.

Siss *nods.*

You *are* free.

Siss *and* **Auntie** *hug. They stand clasped together for a moment, then* **Auntie** *pulls away, trying to hide her tears.*

Off you go. Go on!

Auntie *'shoos'* **Siss** *affectionately.* **Siss** *raises her hand in a goodbye wave and starts back towards the woods. At the edge, she turns to see* **Auntie** *watching.* **Auntie** *raises her hand and waves goodbye.* **Siss** *waves back, slips away.* **Auntie** *waits a moment, looking into the woods after her.*

Scene Ten

Siss's *house.*

Siss *sits over the bowl of water she is about to wash her face in. She stares into it. Her* **Mother** *comes in.*

Mother   Siss?

Siss   Yes?

Mother   Didn't you hear me?

Siss   Sorry.

Mother   What are you doing?

Siss   Nothing.

Mother *looks over her shoulder, down into the water.* **Siss** *pushes her away.*

No, don't.

Mother   Is it so wrong for me to want to look at my daughter's pretty face?

Siss   I don't want us to look in together.

Mother   I hardly recognize you these days.

Siss *is confused.*

Siss   Why?

Mother   You're growing up.

Siss *looks back in the bowl.*

Siss   Do I really have a pretty face?

Mother   You do. Although it could be cleaner.

Siss *laughs. Splashes the water over her face and dries it.*

That's better. I was wondering if you could run an errand for me before school?

Siss   Where?

Mother   Only to the Nedgaard's house. I promised a recipe to Helle's mother.

Siss   Okay. I'd better hurry.

Mother *helps her on with her jacket.*

What's it like outside?

Mother   It's fine.

Siss *looks out of the window.*

Siss   It's windy and raining!

Mother   Can't it be fine all the same?

Siss *laughs.* **Mother** *gives her a slip of paper.*

Siss *sets out on her journey through the wind and rain. On her way through the forest, she meets* **Mats**, *coming the other way.*

Mats   Is that you, Siss?

Siss   Yes.

Mats   Good to see you again.

Siss   And you.

Mats   You look different . . .

Siss   How?

Mats   I don't know . . . more . . .

The two of them are suddenly a little embarrassed.

I don't know.

Beat.

I'm glad to be back on the main road at last! I've been wading up that slope and the drifts are knee-deep. Heavy too, like dragging your legs through wet sand.

Siss   Have you been far?

Mats   To the river.

Siss   All the way down?

Mats   The ice is breaking up.

Siss   What were you doing there?

Mats   Oh . . . just looking around.

Siss *realizes he's been searching.*

You know how it is.

Siss   Yes.
Is the ice palace still standing?

Mats   Not for much longer – a few days maybe and it'll be gone . . . You can see it from a hill near here if you want to . . .

Siss   No. Thanks.

Mats   Sure.
Listen – Siss . . . I've thought of saying something to you. Just . . . if I happen to run into you . . . There's nothing more to be done about it, Siss. You must think about that now.

Siss *stares at her boots.*

I'm sorry.
Look . . . I should get home and change out of these wet things.

Siss *nods. Doesn't look up.*

Don't hide your pretty face, Siss.

Siss *looks up.*

That's better. Goodbye.

Siss   Bye.

Once **Mats** *has disappeared out of sight:*

The most important thing . . . when making your way through the forest . . . is to remember that there is nothing bad at the sides of the road. You walk as fast as you can, and wish at the same time that the road would never end.

The space is suddenly filled with her schoolmates, playing.
They swarm about, taking up positions around her to play 'What's the time Mr Wolf?'.
Torill *is the wolf.*
The children play the game, creeping closer and closer to **Torill**. *Then she calls:*

Torill   Dinnertime!

And they run away. **Siss** *stands still.*

Torill   You're not running.

Siss   I'm not afraid.

Torill   I could catch you.

Siss   I don't think so.

The children creep back, seeing **Torill** *and* **Siss** *together.*

Erik   Are you playing then, Siss?

Siss   No. I'm not.

The others turn away, busy themselves with other games. There is a skipping rope turning, a game of 'catch', clapping songs, and the picking of sides for a game. **Siss** *stands on the edge of all this.*

A boy, **Erik**, *goes and stands nervously next to her. She moves away. After a while he follows her.*

Siss   Is anything the matter?

Erik *nervously spits out his words.*

Erik   It can be as it used to be.

Siss   Do you really believe that?

He thinks.

Erik   No. But it might be possible all the same.

Siss   Who sent you?

Erik   Sent me?

Siss   To say these things to me.

He is obviously hurt.

Erik   I can do some things on my own you know.

Erik *walks off in a huff, back into the heaving crowd.* **Siss** *calls after him, but to no avail. The others continue playing, laughing, with* **Siss** *on the outside. Suddenly she can bear it no longer, summons her courage, and calls out.*

Siss   I have an idea . . .

The playground suddenly stops dead, is silent. **Siss** *is the focus of amazed attention.*

I . . .
You . . .
We . . . should go the ice palace. I heard it's going to fall soon.

A moment of confused silence as the crowd waits for someone to respond. Then, **Inge** *steps forward.*

Inge   D'you really want to go, Siss?

Helle   What'll we do there?

Siss   It might be . . . fun. To see it again before it topples down.

Torill   Are you making fun of us, Siss?

Siss   No . . .

Erik   It's a bit out of the blue.

Torill   But . . .

Torill *looks around the group, sees the eager faces.*

We'll go along.

Torill *makes the promise sign to* **Siss**, *but* **Siss** *does not return it. She starts walking again.*

Siss   The most important thing . . . when making your way through the forest . . .

Mother *comes in.*

Mother   Siss – where are you going?

Siss   To see the ice palace with the others.

Mother   With all your friends?

Siss   They're not my friends . . .

But **Mother** *has linked arms with her, propels her faster through the forest.*

Mother   Oh – Siss! Your father and I have dreamt of this day . . . we've waited so long for you to be happy . . .

Siss   I'm not happy.

Mother   No, of course not. Take care, Siss. Enjoy yourself . . .

And **Mother** *waves, drifts away.* **Siss** *trudges purposefully onwards. The lights dim, the wind gets higher, there is a loud bang!* **Siss** *screams out.* **Mother** *rushes back.*

Mother   What is it?

Siss *is terrified, but keeps moving just the same, faster and faster as the panic mounts.*

Siss   I can't go!

Mother   Why ever not?

Siss   The window . . . I was sleeping and it flew open, all of a sudden, all by itself . . .

Mother   It's just the wind, Siss . . .

Siss   It was so sudden . . .

Mother   Oh, Siss, yesterday, when you told us about this trip – we thought at last this long winter nightmare is over . . .

Siss   I mustn't go.

Mother   Why ever not?

Siss   Something terrible will happen.

Mother   Don't be silly.

Siss   They'll be excited, running about . . .

Mother   Having fun!

Siss   They'll climb onto the palace, onto the icy roof of it! I'll call out that it's dangerous but the roar will be too loud – they won't hear. I'll go after them, huge gaping cracks will appear under our feet . . . the palace will fall . . .

Mother   I promise you nothing bad will happen!

Siss   A promise is only words. It doesn't mean a thing!

Father *enters.*

Father   My, Siss, you're excited about this trip to be up so early! Let's walk a little way together!

He puts his arm around her, urges her onwards. **Mother** *fades away.*

Shall I tell you a secret?

Siss   Something bad?

Father   No! Something good. Very good.

Siss   Okay.

Father   We knew this day would come. When you would be happy again. It wouldn't have been easy to live through this winter otherwise.

He kisses her, then parts from her, waves goodbye.

See you later! I want to hear all about it!

The lights starts to come up again – it's dawn as **Siss** *approaches the fall and stops. It's roaring can be heard in the distance.* **Torill** *appears out of the shadows among the trees.*

Siss   Are you here already?

Torill   I could say the same.

Siss   I wanted to be first.

Torill   I wanted to meet you before the others arrived.

Siss   Well now you've met me.

Siss *turns her back.*

Torill   It was fun to walk home with you yesterday. Everyone thought so.

Siss   Did they?

Torill   Even you, I think.

Siss   Maybe.

Torill   But it hasn't been fun this winter.

Siss   I think I of all people know that.

Torill   The way you treated us.

Siss   It wasn't meant to upset you . . .

Torill   Did you have to stand apart from us in the playground just as she did?

Siss   Don't talk about her!

Torill   We missed her too!

Siss   You don't know what you're saying!

Torill   How do you think that made us feel?

Siss   Right! That's it! If you mention her again, I'll . . .

Siss *points back to the direction she came from.*

Torill   What?

Siss   I'll . . .

Siss *knows she can't leave. The atmosphere calms down a little.*

Torill   Siss?

Torill *holds out her hand to shake* **Siss***'s.*

I'm sorry.

Siss *looks at* **Torill***'s hand. Can't take it.*

Siss   So much that's impossible is happening.

Torill   We're making friends.

Siss   But we mustn't.

Torill   We must.

Siss   No, you mustn't come to me and I must never come to you. And we must never look into a mirror together or it will happen all over again!

Siss *starts to run away.* **Torill** *rushes after her, grabs her, clumsily hugs her.*

Torill   Siss, you mustn't go off and get upset again.

Siss   I know, but . . .

Torill   Are you listening to me?

Siss   Yes.

Torill   Do you understand?

Siss *calms down, lets herself be held by* **Torill** *for a moment. They hear the others arriving.* **Siss** *pushes* **Torill** *away, extends her hand.* **Torill** *shakes it. Suddenly they are surrounded by the others.*

All   Hi Torill!
Hallo Siss!

Inge The sun is so bright today! You can see the palace shining for miles around.

Selma Let's climb it!

Klaus Come on!

They start to move around the fall to find a place on top where they can stand. **Siss** *calls.*

Siss No, it's going to fall soon!

Erik You worry too much, Siss.

Torill Let's go!

Torill *joins the others.* **Siss** *hangs back.*

Siss It isn't safe.

Erik Come on, Siss, it's stood this long. Why should it fall today?

Siss Why shouldn't it?

Erik You know no one can see us here. No one in the world. Don't you think that's a good feeling?

Siss I think we should join the others.

Erik Sure.

When they get to the crevice in the ground that the others have leapt over, he takes her hand and they jump together. They loose hands and join the others in the deafening roar. **Siss** *starts to laugh from the exhilaration. Then there is a terrible crack! And the ice vibrates beneath them. They all scramble desperately for safe ground. Once they know they are all safe, the laughter of relief breaks out. But* **Siss** *does not join in.*

Erik It looks as though you were right, Siss.

Siss *moves away from the group.*

Torill You're not going back, Siss? There's been no harm done . . .

Siss I just want to move a bit further away.

Torill We'll come with you.

Erik Unless you don't want us to . . .

Siss *stops for a second. Looks around her.*

Siss No, come with me.

They hesitate.

Come on!

Siss *heads off again. They follow her down, away from the fall.* **Torill** *runs and overtakes her, heads into a patch of sunlight.*

Torill   Oh!!! Feel this. Come on, Siss. Come into the warm!

Erik *and* **Siss** *join her in the light, soak up the heat, shield their eyes against the sun. Gradually, the light on them fades, comes up on* **Unn**, *watching over the model village. Its orange windows gradually light up.*

Unn *puts her fingers to her lips.*

Unn   Shhh!

Unn *smiles.*

No one can witness the fall of the ice palace. It takes place after all the children are in bed. Safe in their warm homes, sleeping, dreaming. But in the empty half-cold half-light of a spring night like this one, shattered by the pressure of the water, the palace pitches forward into the white froth from the falls. Huge blocks of ice are dashed to pieces, then float away, disappear around a bend in the river, before anyone has woken up or seen a thing. The shattered ice floats on the lower lake, its edges sticking up out of the surface of the water.
It floats and melts, and finally ceases to be.

Unn *watches fondly as a bedside lamp fades up to reveal* **Mother** *tucking a sleepy* **Siss** *into bed.* **Father** *waits in the shadows.*

Mother   Goodnight, Siss.

Siss   Night.

Father   Sleep tight.

Mother *moves to join* **Father** *as* **Siss** *wriggles down under the covers, eyes tightly closed.*

Mother   She'll sleep well after the walk.

Father *nods, hugs* **Mother** *as they both watch over* **Siss**, *plainly relieved that she seems to be looking to the future once again.* **Mother** *turns out the lamp, leaving* **Unn** *alone.*

Unn   It is time, now. It is time.

Unn *savours her last moments, then blows out the lights in the model village. The ice palace is illuminated for a moment, then blacked out as the sound of its final collapse fills the darkness.*

The Mystery at the Heart of Adult Life

Lucinda Coxon interviewed by Jim Mulligan

The Derby Playhouse is where Lucinda Coxon became captivated by the theatre. As a teenager, she spent her days at the local comprehensive school and her evenings and weekends at the theatre. She did some writing at school but when she went to university, the attitude was that you read plays rather than wrote them. But within a month of taking her final examinations, she had written her first play, which was put on in a room over a pub and was a modest success.

'At this point, however, I didn't know how to get on to the next level. Then I joined Loose Exchange. This was a writer-led theatre company with whom I worked on lots of short pieces developed from starting points which we gave one another. It was good experience in that it taught me how important it is to throw away bad plays and have faith in my imagination. I suppose the culmination of this stage of my writing was *Waiting at the Water's Edge*. This is a very big play. It astonishes me now that I wrote it at all. It feels as if it wrote itself. Soon after finishing the play, I approached the director Polly Teale, and the Bush Theatre agreed to house our production. I was incredibly impressed by the way Polly worked. I had directed my first play myself and the experience taught me that directing is a very special skill. At the Bush, I learned to trust the director, and the process confirmed what I like about the theatre, which is that it is collaborative.'

Film scripts and pieces for television followed, with travel to Italy, Romania and New York. And then Lucinda Coxon found *The Ice Palace*, a novel by Tarjei Vesaas, and persuaded the Royal National Theatre to commission her to make a play from it. 'My play is about as close to the original as you can get. As soon as I read a two line summary of the story – it is about two eleven-year-old girls, one of whom gets trapped in a frozen waterfall – I was captivated. I knew it was dramatic. I just wanted to do the best job I could to help the story release itself. I didn't want to impose or interpret.'

What interests Lucinda Coxon is that, although the story is complex and has layers and meanings, it is open: it is a rite-of-passage story that is free of judgment. It is ambiguous and is about ambiguity. The moral, if there is one, is that mystery is not something you are required to put behind you in order to become an adult. You have to learn that mystery is at the heart of adult life and once you have accepted that, you are on the road.

'The play is about life and death and love and loss. Siss never knows where Unn has gone. People have suggested that Unn and Siss are the same person, but I like to read it at a much more literal level. Sometimes, as a child, you may meet someone and just know with absolute certainty that this person will be part of the emotional core of your life. This happens to Siss. It happens very fast and by instinct, and then Unn is gone. She is simply removed, and Siss has to cope with this. She starts to imitate Unn and tries almost to become her, but when Siss stands apart at the edge of the playground, she is imitating. When Unn does this, she understands her own separateness.'

The story is about a child living in her own head. But there is also a picture of a community which works very hard to look after its children. It sometimes gets it wrong, but it wants Siss to be reintegrated into the community. There is a very strong sense of them wanting her back and, in the end, with the help of the community, she has crossed the threshold and become a woman. She owns her experience and is able to go on. Lucinda Coxon is clear that *The Ice Palace* is an open play with no hidden set of meanings. 'People have said it is a play about lesbianism. I simply cannot find that in it. Two eleven-year-old girls take their clothes off together for an instant, and in a sense that is partly sexual, but it is much more about standing in your skin and being vulnerable, being the sum of yourself. It is much more about identity than about sexuality.'

At that first meeting between Siss and Unn, three things happen. They look in the mirror together, they take their clothes off and put them back on very quickly, and Unn says she wants to tell Siss a secret. Siss never learns what the secret is but she knows there is a secret and she is burdened by this. Later on, when Unn is missing and the villagers keep asking Siss if she knows anything, she is trapped because she knows there is something, but not what it is.

'As time goes on, the promise of secrecy gets out of all proportion. The promise was about exclusive friendship and devotion, so when Unn goes missing, Siss tries looking for her, but cannot find her. She then does the sensible thing and stands still, trying to turn herself into a beacon to guide Unn home. If she remains exclusively devoted to Unn, if she keeps their promise sacred, this intimate exchange they have had will guide Unn home. The aunt realizes this, and releases Siss from her promise.'

Usually a stage play will take Lucinda Coxon at least two years to write but *The Ice Palace*, being an adaptation, took only six months. 'It was hard to begin with because I was worried about betraying the novel, about maintaining the integrity of the original, and I was over-polite with it. But once I relaxed, it was enormously pleasurable to work with another writer. It is a very grown-up play, and in the process of writing it I have learned something about growing up.'

Lucinda Coxon was born in Derby. Her plays and films include *Mornings After* (stage play, 1985); *And One Another* (stage play, 1988); *Birdbones* (stage play, 1989); *Improbabilities* (group show of short plays for Loose Exchange Company, 1989); *Eddie's Proposal* (BBC studio screenplay, 1990); *Waiting at the Water's Edge* (stage play, 1992); *Spaghetti Slow* (screenplay, 1993); *Lily and the Secret Planting* (screenplay, 1994); *Wishbones* (stage play, 1995).

The Ice Palace

Production Notes

Setting and staging

The Ice Palace is set in a remote village at the beginning of winter. Cars and phones are not in evidence because this is almost a fairy land; a community that looks after its members.

The staging needs to be fluid, and to suggest the passage of time from the start of winter through the big freeze to the snow's melting and spring's awakening. The playwright recommends an upper and lower stage level, as well as an area dominated by dredging poles, the forest, and the Ice Palace itself. The latter might be suggested by lighting and/or moving figures.

A model village is needed to represent as simply as possible Auntie's house, Siss's bedroom and the classroom. It should be on stage throughout and lit from within. (NB. It is highly recommended that the company has this model throughout the rehearsal period, so that they can build a relationship with it.)

Lighting is an important consideration when suggesting winter: the forest, the moon, shadows, the edge of the lake, the red glow of the sun and the hand-held orange lanterns during the search sequence, against wintry darkness.

Sound, likewise, can suggest the cracking of the ice, dripping water, birds singing, a child's lullaby, footsteps, the river, and distant roaring. As well as recorded sound effects, 'live' vocals can be used to suggest, for example, echoes and a babble of whispered friendship.

Casting

The majority of the cast of twenty-two or more are eleven-year-old classmates. There is the possibility of a certain amount of doubling up, e.g. children and searchers or shadows. The adults, who are positive role models, should ideally be played by older members of the company. Bearing in mind the 'live' vocal effects, it would be good to have a cast with voices of varying pitch. The two main protagonists are Siss and Unn. It's essential that the girls playing these parts have an empathy and can work well together.

Questions

1. How well did Siss fit into the society before she met Unn? Did Unn replace anyone? Who is the more dominant friend?

2. This is a play about life and death, love and loss. What does Siss lose and what does she gain?

3. What would have happened if Unn had shared her secret with Siss? What do you think the secret was? Does our not knowing matter?

4. What effect do spring's arrival and the ice melting have on Siss and her journey back to reality?

5. There is a view (not shared by Lucinda Coxon) that Unn and Siss are the same person. Why might people believe this?

6. How does the loss of Unn affect Siss's relationship with the other children?

7. What is the significance of reflections in the play? For example, the ice, Unn and Siss in the mirror, Unn and Siss themselves.

Exercises

1. Children's games have changed very little over the years and are similar in different countries. Observe children playing in school playgrounds and in the community. Notice the difference between games girls play as opposed to boys. Study the repetitiveness and the rules of the games and recreate some of them.

2. Similarly, listen to the rhymes and chants of the playground. Remember rhymes used when skipping. Use a long skipping-rope to help create group games and rhymes. Experiment by speeding up the pace of the skipping, and slowing it down. Manipulate the rope to exclude or welcome specific individuals. Try skipping in pairs, threes, or more simultaneously.

3. Take one or more childhood songs and use them as a vocal warm-up at each rehearsal. Sing softly, with vigour, in parts, sing in a circle and then while moving around the space.

4. As a group, improvise bird-song – one person starts and, one by one, the others join in. Imagine you are creating a dawn chorus, gradually followed by the birds falling silent.

5. As an ensemble, turn yourselves into a search party: one person is joined by another, then another, and the group's leader and the direction taken change. Improvise giving instructions and the excitement of a seemingly successful outcome, followed by the disappointment of failure. Repeat the exercise using hand-held torches. See how little more is required to tell the same scenario while relying on the lights.

6. Choose an echoey room or other location – a cave, a shower-room, a gallery, a disused swimming pool? Experiment with whispers and echoes. Have one member of the group volunteer to be guided around the space by whispers only. Now follow this through to the scene in the play where Unn enters the ice palace.

Suzy Graham-Adriani
Director/Producer for BT National Connections

The Dark Tower

Louis MacNeice

.

Introductory Note

The Dark Tower is a parable play, belonging to that wide class of writings which includes *Everyman, The Faerie Queene* and *The Pilgrim's Progress.* Though under the name of allegory this kind of writing is sometimes dismissed as outmoded, the clothed as distinct from the naked allegory is in fact very much alive. Obvious examples are *Peer Gynt* and the stories of Kafka but also in such books as *The Magic Mountain* by Thomas Mann, where the disguise of 'realism' is maintained and nothing happens that is quite inconceivable in life, it is still the symbolic core which makes the work important. My own impression is that pure 'realism' is in our time almost played out, though most works of fiction of course will remain realistic *on the surface.* The single-track mind and the single-plane novel or play are almost bound to falsify the world in which we live. The fact that there is method in madness and fact that there is fact in fantasy (and equally fantasy in 'fact') have been brought home to us not only by Freud and other psychologists but by events themselves. This being so, reportage can no longer masquerade as art. So the novelist, abandoning the 'straight' method of photography, is likely to resort once more not only to the twist of plot but to all kinds of other twists which may help him to do justice to the world's complexity. Some element of parable therefore, far from making a work thinner and more abstract, ought to make it more concrete. Man does after all live by symbols.

The dual-plane work will not normally be allegory in the algebraic sense; i.e. it will not be desirable or even possible to equate each of the outward and visible signs with a precise or rational inner meaning. Thus *The Dark Tower* was suggested to me by Browning's poem 'Childe Roland to the Dark Tower came', a work which does not admit of a completely rational analysis and still less adds up to any clear moral or message. This poem has the solidity of a dream; the writer of such a poem, though he may be aware of the 'meanings' implicit in his dream, must not take the dream to pieces, must present his characters concretely, must allow the story to persist as a story and not dwindle into a diagram. While I could therefore have offered here an explicit summary of those implicit 'meanings' in *The Dark Tower* of which I myself was conscious, I am not doing so, because it might impair the impact of the play. I would merely say – for the benefit of people like the *Daily Worker*'s radio critic, who found the programme pointless and depressing – that in my opinion it is neither. *The Faerie Queene, The Pilgrim's Progress, Piers Plowman* and the early Moralities could not have been written by men without any beliefs. In an age which precludes the simple and militant faith of a Bunyan, belief (whether consciously formulated or not) still remains a *sine qua non* of the creative writer. I have my beliefs and they permeate *The Dark Tower.* But do not ask me what 'Ism' it illustrates or what solution it offers. You do not normally ask for such things in the single-plane work; why should they be forced upon something much more complex? 'Why, look you now, how unworthy a thing you make of me!' What is life *useful* for anyway?

Characters

Sergeant-Trumpeter
Gavin
Roland
Mother
Tutor
Sylvie
Blind Peter
Soak
Steward
Neaera
Ship's Officer
Priest
Roland's Father
Parrot
Raven
Clock Voice

Opening Announcement

The Dark Tower. The programme which follows is a parable play – suggested by Robert Browning's poem 'Childe Roland to the Dark Tower came'. The theme is the ancient but evergreen theme of the Quest – the dedicated adventure; the manner of presentation is that of a dream – but a dream that is full of meaning. Browning's poem ends with a challenge blown on a trumpet:

> And yet
> Dauntless the slughorn to my lips I set
> And blew. 'Childe Roland to the Dark Tower came'.

Note well the words 'And yet'. Roland did not have to – he did not wish to – and yet in the end he came to: The Dark Tower.

A trumpet plays through the Challenge Call.

Sergeant-Trumpeter
There now, that's the challenge. And mark this:
Always hold the note at the end.

Gavin
Yes, Sergeant-Trumpeter, yes.

Roland (*as a boy*)
Why need Gavin hold the note at the end?

Sergeant-Trumpeter
Ach, you're too young to know. It's all tradition.

Roland
What's tradition, Sergeant-Trumpeter?

Gavin
Ask Mother that one. (*With a half-laugh.*)
She knows.

Sergeant-Trumpeter
Aye, *she* knows.
But run along, sonny. Leave your brother to practise.

The trumpet re-begins – breaks off.

Again.

The trumpet re-begins and is sustained.

That's it now. But hold that last note – hold it!

On the long last note the trumpet fades into the distance.

Roland
Mother! What's tradition?

Mother
Hand me that album. No – the black one.

Roland
Not the locked one!

Mother
Yes, the locked one. I have the key.
Now, Roland, sit here by me on the sofa.
We'll look at them backwards.

Roland
Why must we look at them backwards?

Mother
Because then you may recognize –
Now! You know who this is?

Roland
Why, that's my brother Michael.
And here's my brother Henry! ·
Michael and Henry and Denis and Roger and John!
(*He speaks with the bright callousness of children.*)
Do you keep this album locked because they're dead?

Mother
No, not exactly.
Now – can you guess who this is?

Roland
That's someone I saw in a dream once.

Mother
It must have been in a dream
He left this house three months before you were born.

Roland
Is it . . . is it my father?

Mother
Yes. And this is your grandfather. And this is *his* father –
For the time being you needn't look at the rest;
This book goes back through seven long generations
As far as George, the founder of the family.

Roland
And did they all die the same way?

Mother
They did, Roland. And now I've answered your question.

Roland
What question, Mother?

The trumpet call is heard in the distance.

Ah, there's Gavin practising.
He's got it right at last.

The call ends and **Gavin** *appears.*

Gavin (*excited*)
Mother! I know the challenge. When can I leave? Tomorrow?

Mother
Why not today, Gavin?

Gavin
Today! But I haven't yet checked my equipment;
I mean – for such a long journey I –

Mother
You will travel light, my son.

Gavin
Well, yes . . . of course . . . today then.

Roland
Where are you going, Gavin?

Gavin
Why, surely you know; I'm –

Mother
Hsh!

Roland
I know where he's going. Across the sea like Michael.

Gavin
That's right, Roland. Across the big, bad sea.
Like Michael and Henry and Denis and Roger and John.
And after that through the Forest.
And after that through the Desert –

Roland
What's the Desert made of?

Gavin
Well . . . I've never been there.
Some deserts are made of sand and some are made of grit but –

Mother (*as if to herself*)
This one is made of doubts and dried-up hopes.

Roland (*still bright*)
And what do you find at the other end of the desert?

Gavin
Well, I . . . well . . .

Mother
You can tell him.

Gavin
I find the Dark Tower.

The Dark Tower theme gives a musical transition to the schoolroom.

Tutor
Now, Master Roland, as this is our first day of lessons
I trust I shall find you as willing a pupil
As your six brothers before you.

Roland
Did you like teaching my brothers?

Tutor
Like it? It was an honour.
It was teaching to some purpose.

Roland
When's my brother Gavin coming back?

Tutor
What!

Roland
Gavin. When's he coming back?

Tutor
Roland! . . .
I see I must start from the beginning.
I thought your mother had told you but maybe being the youngest –

Roland
What would my mother have told me?

Tutor
You ask when your brother Gavin is coming back?
You must get this straight from the start:
Your family never come back.

Roland *begins to interrupt.*

Tutor
Now, now, now, don't let me scare you.
Sit down on that stool and I'll try to explain.
Now, Roland –
I said that to teach your brothers was an honour.
Before your mother engaged me to tutor John
I was an usher in a great city,
I taught two dozen lads in a class –
The sons of careerists – salesmen, middlemen, half-men,
Governed by greed and caution; it was my job
To teach them enough – and only enough –
To fit them for making money. Means to a means.
But with your family it is a means to an end.

Roland (*naively puzzled*)
My family don't make money?

Tutor
They make history

Roland
And what do you mean by an end?

Tutor
I mean – surely they told you?
I mean: the Dark Tower.

Roland
Will *I* ever go to the Dark Tower?

Tutor
Of course you will. That is why I am here.

Roland (*gaily*)
Oh well! That's different!

Tutor
It is.

Roland
And that means I'll fight the Dragon?

Tutor
Yes – but let me tell you:
We call it the Dragon for short, it is a nameless force
Hard to define – for no one who has seen it,
Apart from those who have seen its handiwork,
Has returned to give an account of it.
All that we know is there is something there
Which makes the Dark Tower dark and is the source

Of evil through the world. It is immortal
But men must try to kill it – and keep on trying
So long as we would be human.

Roland
What would happen
If we just let it alone?

Tutor
Well . . . some of us would live longer; all of us
Would lead a degraded life, for the Dragon would be supreme
Over our minds as well as our bodies. Gavin –
And Michael and Henry and Denis and Roger and John –
Might still be here – perhaps your fathr too,
He would be seventy-five – but mark this well:
They would not be themselves. Do you understand?

Roland
I'm not quite sure, I . . .

Tutor
You are still small. We'll talk of the Dragon later.
Now come to the blackboard and we'll try some Latin.
You see this sentence?

Roland
Per ardua . . .

Tutor
Per ardua ad astra.

Roland
What does it mean?

Tutor
It does not go very well in a modern language.
We had a word 'honour' – but it is obsolete.
Try the word 'duty'; and there's another word –
'Necessity'.

Roland
Necessity! That's a bit hard to spell.

Tutor
You'll have to spell it, I fear. Repeat this after me:
N –

Roland
N –

Tutor

–

Roland

–

As they spell it through, their voices dwindle away and a tolling bell grows up out of the distance.

Sergeant-Trumpeter
Ah God, there's the bell for Gavin.
He had the greatest power to his lungs of the lot of them.
And now he's another name in the roll of honour
Where Michael's is still new gold. Five years it is –
Or would it be more like six – since we tolled for Michael?
Bells and trumpets, trumpets and bells,
I'll have to be learning the young one next;
Then he'll be away too and my lady will have no more.

Mother (*coldly; she has come up behind him*)
No more children, Sergeant-Trumpeter?

Sergeant-Trumpeter
Och, I beg your pardon. I didn't see you.

Mother
No matter. But know this:
I have one more child to bear.
No, I'm not mad; you needn't stare at me, Sergeant.
This is a child of stone.

Sergeant-Trumpeter
A child of. . . ?

Mother
Stone. To be born on my death-bed.
No matter. I'm speaking in metaphor.

Sergeant-Trumpeter (*relieved to change the subject*)
That's all right then. How's young Roland
Making out at his lessons?

Mother
I don't know. Roland lacks concentration; he's not like my other sons,
He's almost flippant, he's always asking questions –

Sergeant-Trumpeter
Och, he's young yet.

Mother
Gavin was his age once.
So were Michael and Henry and Denis and Roger and John.
They never forgot what they learnt. And they asked no questions.

Sergeant-Trumpeter
Ah well – by the time that Roland comes to me
When he's had his fill of theory and is all set for action,
In another half dozen years when he comes to learn the trumpet call –

Mother
Hsh, don't talk of it now.
(*As if to herself.*)
Let one bell toll at a time.

The bell recedes into nothing, covering a passage of years. **Roland** *is now grown up.*

Tutor
So ends our course on ethics. Thank you, Roland;
After all these years our syllabus is concluded.
You have a brain; what remains to be tried is your will.
Remember our point today: the sensitive man
Is the more exposed to seduction. In six years
I have come to know you; you have a warm heart –
It is perhaps too warm for a man with your commission,
Therefore be careful. Keep to your one resolve,
Your single code of conduct, listen to no one
Who doubts your values – and above all, Roland,
Never fall in love – That is not for you.
If ever a hint of love should enter your heart,
You must arise and go. . . . That's it: Go!
Yes, Roland my son. Go quickly.

His last words fade slightly and **Sylvie***'s voice fades in.*

Sylvie
But why must you go so quickly? Now that the sun's come out.

Roland
I have my lesson to learn.

Sylvie
You're always learning lessons!
I'll begin to think you prefer your books to me.

Roland
Oh, but Sylvie, this isn't books any more.

Sylvie
Not books? Then –

Roland
I'm learning to play the trumpet.

Sylvie (*irritated*)
Whatever for? Roland, you make me laugh.
Is this another idea of your mother's?
I needn't ask. What's all this leading to?

Roland (*quietly*)
I could tell you, darling. But not today.
Today is a thing in itself – apart from the future.
Whatever follows, I will remember this tree
With this dazzle of sun and shadow – and I will remember
The mayflies jigging above us in the delight
Of the dying instant – and I'll remember *you*
With the bronze lights in your hair.

Sylvie
Yes, darling; but why so sad?
There will be other trees and –

Roland
Each tree is itself, each moment is itself,
Inviolable gifts of time . . . of God –
But you cannot take them with you.

Sylvie
Take them with you where?

Roland
Kiss me, Sylvie. I'm keeping my teacher waiting.

The Challenge Call is played through once.

Sergeant-Trumpeter
Nicely blown! Nicely blown!
You've graduated, my lad.
But remember – when I'm not here – hold the note at the end.

Roland (*a shade bitter*)
You mean when *I'm* not here.

Sergeant-Trumpeter
Aye, you're right. But you are my last pupil,
I'll be shutting up shop, I want you to do me credit.
When you've crossed the sea and the desert and come to the place itself
I want you to do me credit when you unsling that horn.

Roland
I hope I will.
(*He pauses; then slightly embarrassed.*)
Sergeant?

Sergeant-Trumpeter
Eh?

Roland
Do you think that there really is any dragon to fight?

Sergeant-Trumpeter
What are you saying! What was it killed Gavin?
And Michael and Henry and Denis and Roger and John,
And your father himself and his father before him and all of them back to
    George!

Roland
I don't know but . . . nobody's *seen* the dragon.

Sergeant-Trumpeter
Seen him? They've seen what he's done!
Have you never talked to Blind Peter?
I thought not. Cooped up here in the castle –
Inside this big black ring of smothering yew-trees –
You never mixed with the folk.
But before you leave – if you want a reason for leaving –
I recommend that you pay a call on Peter.
And his house is low; mind your head as you enter.

Another verbal transition.

Blind Peter (*old and broken*)
That's right, sir; mind your head as you enter.
Now take that chair, it's the only one with springs,
I saved it from my heyday. Well now, sir,
It's kind of you to visit me. I can tell
By your voice alone that you're your father's son;
Your handshake's not so strong though.

Roland
Why, was my father – ?

Blind Peter
He had a grip of iron.
And what's more, sir, he had a will of iron.
And what's still more again, he had a conscience –
Which is something we all need. *I* should know!

Roland
Why?

Blind Peter
Why what?

Roland
Why do you sound so sad when you talk about having a
conscience?

Blind Peter
Because his conscience is something a man can lose.
It's cold in here, I'll make a long story short.
Fifty years ago when I had my sight –
But the Dragon was loose at the time –
I had a job and a wife and a new-born child
And I believed in God. Until one day –
I told you the Dragon was loose at the time,
No one had challenged him lately; so he came out from his den –
What some people call the Tower – and creeping around
He got to our part of the world; nobody saw him of course,
There was just like a kind of a bad smell in the air
And everything went sour; people's mouths and eyes
Changed their look overnight – and the government changed too –
And as for me I woke up feeling different
And when I looked in the mirror that first morning
The mirror said 'Informer'!

Roland (*startled*)
Informer?

Blind Peter
Yes, sir. My new role.
They passed a pack of laws forbidding this and that
And anyone breaking 'em – the penalty was death.
I grew quite rich sending men to their death.
The last I sent was my wife's father.

Roland
But . . . but did you believe in these laws?

Blind Peter
Believe? Aha! Did I believe in anything?
God had gone round the corner. I was acquiring riches.
But to make a long story short –
When they hanged my wife's father my wife took poison,
So I was left with the child. Then the child took ill –
Scared me stiff – so I sent for all the doctors,
I could afford 'em then – but they couldn't discover
Anything wrong in its body, it was more as if its soul
Was set on quitting – and indeed why not?
To be a human being, people agree, is difficult.

Roland
Then the child. . . ?

Blind Peter
Quit.
Yes; she quit – but slowly.
I watched it happen. That's why I'm blind.

Roland
Why? You don't mean you yourself –

Blind Peter
When you've seen certain things, you don't want to see no more.
Tell me, sir. Are people's faces nowadays
As ugly as they were? You know what I mean: evil?

Roland
No, not most of them. *Some*, I suppose –

Blind Peter
Those ones belong to the Dragon.

Roland (*exasperated*)
Why put the blame of everything on the Dragon?
Men have free choice, haven't they?
Free choice of good or evil –

Blind Peter
That's just it –
And the evil choice is the Dragon!
But I needn't explain it to you, sir; *you've* made up your mind,
You're like your father – one of the dedicated
Whose life is a quest, whose death is a victory.
Yes! God bless you! *You've* made up your mind!

Roland (*slowly and contemplatively*)
But have I, Peter? Have I?

Verbal transition.

Sylvie
Have you, Roland dearest? Really made up your mind?

Roland (*without expression*)
I go away today.

Sylvie
That's no answer.
You go away because they tell you to.
Because your mother's brought you up on nothing
But out-of-date beliefs and mock heroics.
It's easy enough for her –

Roland (*indignantly*)
Easy for her?
Who's given her flesh and blood – and I'm the seventh son!

Sylvie
I've heard all that. They call it sacrifice
But each new death is a stone in a necklace to her.
Your mother, Roland, is mad.

Roland (*with quiet conviction*)
The world is mad.

Sylvie
Not all of it, my love. Those who have power
Are mad enough but there *are* people, Roland,
Who keep themselves to themselves or rather to each other,
Living a sane and gentle life in a forest nook or a hill pocket,
Perpetuating their kind and their kindness, keeping
Their hands clean and their eyes keen, at one with
Themselves, each other and nature. I had thought
That you and I perhaps –

Roland
There is no perhaps
In my tradition, Sylvie.

Sylvie
You mean in your family's.
Isn't it time you saw that you were different?
You're no knight errant, Roland.

Roland
No, I'm not.
But there is a word 'Necessity' –

Sylvie
Necessity? You mean your mother's orders.

Roland (*controlled*)
Not quite. But apart from that,
I saw a man today – they call him Blind Peter –

Sylvie
Leave the blind to mislead the blind. That Peter
Is where he is because of his own weakness;
You can't help him, Roland.

Roland
Maybe not – (*With sudden insight.*)
But maybe I can do something to prevent
A recurrence of Blind Peters.

Sylvie
Imagination!

Roland
Imagination? . . . That things can be bettered?
That action can be worthwhile? That there are ends
Which, even if not reached, are worth approaching?
Imagination? Yes, I wish I had it –
I have a little – You should support that little
And not support my doubts.
(*A drum-roll is heard.*)
Listen; there is the drum.
They are waiting for me at the gate.
Sylvie, I –

Sylvie
Kiss me at least.

Pause.

Roland
I shall never –

Sylvie
See me again?
You will, Roland, you will.
I know you. You will set out but you won't go on,
Your common sense will triumph, you'll come back.
And your love for me will triumph in the end –

Roland
This is the end. Goodbye.

The drum swells and ends on a peak. This is the Scene of Departure.

Tutor
To you, Roland, my last message:
For seven years I have been your tutor.
You have worked hard on the whole but whether really
You have grasped the point of it all remains to be seen.
A man lives on a sliding staircase –
Sliding downwards, remember; to be a man
He has to climb against it, keeping level
Or even ascending slightly; he will not reach
The top – if there is a top – and when he dies
He will slump and go down regardless. All the same
While he lives he must climb. Remember that.
And I thank you for your attention. Goodbye, Roland.

Sergeant-Trumpeter
To you, Roland, my last message:
You are off now on the Quest like your brothers before you
To take a slap at the Evil that never dies.
Well, here's this trumpet; sling it around your waist
And keep it bright and clean till the time comes
When you have to sound the challenge – the first and the last time –
And I trust you will do your old instructor credit
And put the fear of God – or of Man – into that Dragon.
That's all now. God bless you. But remember –
Hold that note at the end.

Mother
To you, Roland, my last message:
Here is a ring with a blood-red stone. So long as
This stone retains its colour, it means that I
Retain my purpose in sending you on the Quest.
I put it now on your finger.

Roland
Mother! It burns.

Mother
That is the heat of the stone. So long as the stone is red
The ring will burn and that small circle of fire
Around your little finger will be also
The circle of my will around your mind.
I gave a ring like this to your father, Roland,
And to John and Roger and Denis and Henry and Michael
And to Gavin the last before you. My will was around and behind him.
Should ever you doubt or waver, look at this ring –
And feel it burn – and go on.

Roland
Mother! Before I go –

Mother
No more words. Go!
Turn your face to the sea.
(*Raising her voice.*)
Open the gates there!
(*Aside.*)
The March of Departure, Sergeant.
Let my son go out – my last. And make the music gay!

*The March begins at full volume, then gradually dwindles as **Roland** and the listener move away. By the time the music has vanished **Roland** has reached the Port, where he addresses a stranger.*

Roland
Forgive me stopping you, sir –

Soak (*old, alcoholic, leering*)
Forgive you? Certainly not.
I'm on my way to the Tavern.

Roland
I'm on my way to the quays. Is it this turning or next?

Soak
Any turning you like. Look down these stinking streets –
There's sea at the end of each of 'em.
Yes, young man, but what's at the end of the sea?
Never believe what they said when you booked your passage.

Roland
But I haven't booked it yet.

Soak
Not booked your passage yet! Why, then there's no need to hurry.
You come with me to the Tavern; it's only a step.

Roland
I cannot spare a step

Soak
All right, all right;
If you won't come to the Tavern, the Tavern must come to you.
Ho there, music!

The orchestra strikes up raggedly – continuing while he speaks.

That's the idea. Music does wonders, young man.
Music can build a palace, let alone a pub.
Come on, you masons of the Muses, swing it,
Fling me up four walls. Now, now, don't drop your tempo;
Easy with those hods. All right; four walls.
Now benches – tables – No! No doors or windows.
What drunk wants daylight? But you've left out the bar.
Come on – 'Cellos! Percussion! All of you! A bar!
That's right. Dismiss!

The music ends.

Soak
Barmaid.

Barmaid
Yes, sir?

Soak
Give us whatever you have and make it triple.

Roland
Just a small one for me, please.

Soak
Oh don't be so objective. One would think,
Looking at your long face, that there's a war on.

Roland
But –

Soak
There is no war on – and you have no face.
Drink up. Don't be objective.

Roland
What in the name of – ?

Barmaid
Look, dearie; don't mind *him*.
He always talks like that. You take my tip;
You're new here and this town is a seaport,
The tone is rather. . . . You go somewhere inland.

Roland
But how can I?
I have to go to sea.

Barmaid (*seriously*)
The sea out there leads nowhere.

Soak
Come, sweetheart, the same again.

Barmaid
Nowhere, I've warned you.
(*In a whisper.*) As for our friend here,
Don't stay too long in his company.

Soak
What's that? Don't stay too long in my what?

Barmaid
Company is the word.

Soak
Company? I have none. Why, how could I?
There's never anyone around where I am.
I exist for myself and all the rest is projection.
Come on, projection, drink! Dance on your strings and drink!

Barmaid
Oblige him, dearie, oblige him.

Soak
There! My projection drinks.
I wrote this farce before I was born, you know –
This puppet play. In my mother's womb, dear boy –
I have never abdicated the life of the womb.
Watch, Mabel: my new puppet drinks again –
A pretty boy but I've given him no more lines.
Have I, young man?

Pause.

You see, he cannot speak.
All he can do henceforward is to drink –
Look! A pull on the wire – the elbow lifts.
Give him the same again.

Barmaid
Well . . .

Soak
There is no well about it. Except the well
That has no bottom and that fills the world.
Triplets, I said. Where are those damned musicians?
Back up, you puppets! Play!

The orchestra strikes up a lullaby, continued behind his speech.

Soak (*sleepily*)
Good. Serenade me now till I fall asleep
And all the notes are one – and all the sounds are silence.
Unity, Mabel, unity is my motto.
The end of drink is a whole without any parts –
A great black sponge of night that fills the world
And when you squeeze it, Mabel, it drips inwards.
D'you want me to squeeze it? Right. Piano there.
Piano – I must sleep. Didn't you hear me?
Piano, puppets. All right, pianissimo.
Nissimo . . . nissimo . . . issimo. . . .

The music ends and only his snoring is heard.

Roland
A puppet? . . . A projection? . . . How he lies!
And yet I've sometimes thought the same, you know –
The same but the other way round.
There is no evidence for anything
Except my own existence – he says his.

But he's wrong anyway – look at him snoring there.
If I were something existing in his mind
How could I go on now that he's asleep?

Soak (*muffled*)
Because I'm dreaming you.

Roland
Dreaming?

Barmaid
Yes, sir.
He does have curious dreams.

Soak
Yes, and the curious things about my dreams
Is that they always have an unhappy ending
For all except the dreamer. Thus at the moment
You'd never guess, young man, what role I've cast you for –

Roland
What the – ?

Barmaid
Never mind, dear.
Tomorrow he'll wake up.

Roland
Tomorrow *he'll* wake up?
And I – Shall I wake up? Perhaps to find
That this whole Quest is a dream. Perhaps I'm still at home
In my bed by the window looking across the valley
Between the yew-trees to where Sylvie lives
Not among yews but apples –

He is interrupted by a terrific voice crashing in on the 'Bar' from the outer world.

Stentor
All Aboard!

Roland
What's that?

Stentor
All Aboard!

Soak
You'd never guess
What happens in my dream. . . .

Stentor
All Aboard! All Aboard!
Come along there, young man – unless you want to be left.
All Aboard for the Further Side of the Sea,
For the Dead End of the World and the Borne of No Return!

The noise of a crowd materializes, increasing.

All Aboard, ladies and gents, knaves and fools, babes and sucklings,
Philistines, pharisees, parasites, pimps,
Nymphos and dipsos – All Aboard!
Lost souls and broken bodies; make it snappy.
That's right, folks. Mind your feet on the gangway.

Through the racket of gardarening passengers is heard the mechanical voice of the **Ticket Collector**.

Ticket Collector
Ticket? Thank you . . . Ticket? Thank you . . . Ticket?
Thank you . . . Ticket? Thank you . . .

The crowd noises fade out; **Roland** *is now below decks.*

Steward (*with an 'off-straight' accent*)
This way, sir. Let me show you your stateroom.
Hot and cold and a blue light over the bed.
Ring once for a drink, twice for an aspirin.
Now if you want anything else – a manicure, for example –

Roland
No, steward. A sleeping draught.

Steward (*archly*)
Sir! In the morning?

Roland
Morning be damned. My head aches.

Steward
Drinking last night, sir?

Roland
Thinking.

Steward (*rattling it off*)
Thinking? That's too bad, sir.
But you'll soon get over that, sir.
In this shop nobody thinks, sir.
Why should they? They're at sea, sir . . .
And if your brain's at sea, sir –

Roland (*angrily*)
Listen! I want a sleeping draught.
How many times do I have to ring for that?

Steward (*unperturbed*)
As many times as you like, sir.
If you can keep awake, sir.
(*Pimpishly.*)
But talking of sleeping draughts, sir,
Do you hear that lady playing the fiddle?

Roland
Fiddle? No. I don't.

Steward
Ah, that's because she plays it in her head.
But she's a very nice lady, sir.
Her name, sir, is Neaera.

Roland
Why should I care what her name is?
I tell you, steward –

Steward
Of course if you'd rather play tombola –

Roland
Tombola?

Steward (*throwing it away*)
Game of chance, sir. They call out numbers.
Kills the time, sir. Rather like life, sir.
You can buy your tickets now in the lounge.
The ship's started, you know, sir.

Roland
Oh, so the ship's started? (*Worried.*)
But I can't hear the engines.

Steward
Can't you, sir? I was right then.

Roland
Right? What do you mean?

Steward
I thought so the moment I saw you.
You don't, sir; of course you don't.

Roland
Don't what, damn you? Don't what?

Steward
You don't know where you're going, sir.

The ship's engines are heard on the orchestra; from them emerges the chatter of the lounge with the banal laughter of tombola players.

Officer
Clickety-click; sixty-six . . .
Kelly's Eye: Number One . . .
And we –

Crowd (*raggedly*)
Shake the Bag!

The orchestral engines give place to a solo violin.

Neaera (*to herself, velvety*)
. . . Andantino . . . rallentando . . . adagio –
(*Her violin playing breaks off. Foreign accent.*)
Mon Dieu! You startled me.

Roland
I'm sorry, I –

Neaera (*cooingly*)
Do sit down. So you're going Nowhere too?

Roland
On the contrary, Madam –

Neaera
Call me Neaera.

Roland
But –

Neaera
And I'll call you Roland.

Roland
How do you know my name?

Neaera
A little bird told me. A swan, if you want to know;
He sang your name and he died.
That's right, sit down. I've seen your dossier too.

Roland
Seen my –

Neaera
Oh yes, chéri. In the Captain's cabin.

Roland
But how can I have a dossier? I've done nothing.

Neaera
That's just it. It's dull.
But the future part amuses me.
Oh yes, my dear, this dossier includes the future –
And you don't come out of it well.

Roland
What do you mean?

Neaera
You never believed in this Quest of yours, you see –
The Dark Tower – the Dragon – all this blague.
That's why you were so easy to seduce
In the idle days at sea – the days that are just beginning.

Her violin begins again, then gives way to the lounge chatter, covering a passage of time.

Officer
Key of the Door: Twenty-One!
Eleventh Hour: Eleven!
Ten Commandments: Nine!
Kelly's Eye: Number One!
And we –

Crowd
Shake the bag!

The violin re-emerges.

Neaera
. . . Lento . . . accelerando . . . presto . . . calando . . .
morendo. . . .

The violin fades away: it is meant to have established an affaire between **Roland** *and*
Neaera

Steward (*slyly*)
Well, sir? So the lady is still practising.
Golden days, sir, golden days.
At sea, sir, have you noticed,
One doesn't notice time?
You probably feel you just came on board yesterday
And yet you got your sea-legs weeks ago, sir.

Roland
Sea-legs? Why, this trip has been so calm
I've never felt –

Steward
That's right, sir; never feel.
There's nothing in life but profit and pleasure.
Allegro assai – some people plump for pleasure
But I now fancy the profit – (*Receiving a tip.*)
Ah thank you, sir, thank you.
The sea today in the sun, sir, looks like what shall I say, sir?

Roland
The sea today? A dance of golden sovereigns.

Neaera
The sea today is adagios of doves.

Roland
The sea today is gulls and dolphins.

Neaera
The sea today is noughts and crosses.

Officer (*cutting in rapidly*)
And we –

Crowd
Shake the bag!

Neaera
The sea today, Roland, is crystal.

Roland
The sea today, Neaera, is timeless.

Neaera
The sea today is drums and fifes.

Roland
The sea today is broken bottles.

Neaera
The sea today is snakes and ladders.

Officer (*as before*)
Especially snakes!

Crowd
Especially snakes!

Neaera (*wheedling*)
Roland, what's that ring? I've never seen one like it.

Roland
There is no other ring like it.

Neaera
A strange ring for a man . . .
My colour, you know – that red . . .
Why do you twitch your finger?

Roland
Because it burns.

Neaera
It burns?
Like tingling ears perhaps? Someone is thinking of you.

Roland (*startled – and suddenly depressed.*)
What? . . . I hope not. (*Changing the subject.*)
Come, darling, let's have a drink.

Officer
And we –

Crowd
Shake the Bag!

Roland
The sea today is drunken marble.

Neaera
The sea today is silver stallions.

Roland
The sea today is – Tell me, steward:
Where's all this floating seaweed come from?

Steward
I imagine, sir – forgive me mentioning it –
That we are approaching land.

Roland
Land!

Steward
Yes, sir – but *you* won't be landing of course.
The best people never land, sir.

Roland (*to himself, fatalistically*)
No? . . .
I suppose not.

Neaera's *violin is heard again.*

Neaera (*to herself*)
. . . piu sonoro . . . con forza . . . accelerando . . .
crescendo. . . .

The orchestra is added for a final crashing chord and at once we hear the hubbub of a crowd.

Stentor
Anyone more for the shore? Anyone more for the shore?
Line up there on the forward deck
All that wants to chance their neck!
Anyone more for the shore?

Ticket Collector
This way: thank you – This way: thank you –
This way: thank you – This way: thank you.

Stentor
Anyone more? Hurry up please!
But remember this: Once you're off
You can't come back, not ever, on board.
We leave at once. At once!

Ticket Collector ·
This way: thank you – This way: thank you – This way: thank
you – This way: thank you.

First Passenger (*cockney*)
Here, here, who're you shoving? What's the blinkin' hurry?

His Wife
That's right.

First Passenger
Some people seem very keen to land in the future.
Can't use their eyes – if you ask me!

His Wife
That's right. Look at them vicious rocks.

First Passenger
And that tumbledown shack that thinks it's a Customs House.

His Wife
And them horrible mountains behind it.

Second Passenger (*northern*)
You'd think this country was uninhabited.

Ticket Collector
This way: thank you – This way: thank you –
(*With finality.*)
This way: thank *you*!
(*Wearily.*)
OK, sir. That's the lot.

Stentor
Gangway up! Gangway up!
Clear away there. Mind your heads!

Neaera
What are you staring at, Roland?
Come away, chéri; the show's over.
There goes the gangway; we're moving out now.
What *are* you staring at, darling?

Roland (*to himself*)
Was that . . . was that . . . I couldn't see in the face of the
sun but –
Steward, you've sharp eyes.
Did you see over there on the quay, sitting on a rusty
bollard –

Steward
Hsh, sir, Neaera will hear you.
Yes, sir, a very nice piece.
She was looking at you, sir, too – staring in fact, one might say.
Seems to be staring still – but what's she doing now?
Climbing up on the bollard?
Good Lord, sir, that's bad form; she's making gestures.

Sylvie (*distant cry*)
Roland! . . . Roland! . . .

Roland
Sylvie!
I knew it. Out of my way there!

Stentor
Here, here, here! Stop him!
Man gone mad there! Don't let him jump!

General commotion.

Neaera
Roland! Come back!

A loud splash.

Stentor
Man overboard! Man overboard!

The crowd reacts excitedly.

Lifebuoy! Where's the lifebuoy?

Voice
Garn! This here ship don't carry no lifebuoys.
Nor he won't need one. Look! He's climbing up on the quay.

Engines start up again.

Officer (*triumphantly*)
And we –

Crowd
Shake the Bag!

Neaera (*now revealing her hardness*)
Well, James . . . That's that.

Steward
Yes, madam.

Neaera
You can drop the madam now.

Steward
Yes, Neaera – my sweetie-pie.

Neaera (*matter-of-fact*)
That's more like it, James, my great big he-man.
Come to my cabin now; we'll count the takings.

The fading engines take the liner to sea; **Roland** *is left on the Shore, with* **Sylvie** *sobbing.*

Roland (*dead-pan*)
There she goes now.

Sylvie (*echoing him*)
There she goes now . . . (*Then bursting out.*)
Roland, you are a hypocrite!

Roland (*quietly – but ashamed*)
No, Sylvie; merely a sleepwalker.
Ugh! (*He shivers.*)

Sylvie (*calm again*)
The sea must have been cold. Come, let's walk.

Roland
How did you get here, Sylvie?

Sylvie (*a shade bitter*)
I followed you – but not on a luxury liner.
Mine was a cargo boat, its limit was seven knots.

Roland
And yet you got here first.
And now I suppose you regret it.
Are you going to leave me, Sylvie?

Sylvie
How can I? We're marooned here.
This is a desolate land.
(*With forced control.*)
I suggest we keep together.

Roland
You have the gift of forgiveness.

Sylvie
I have the gift of common sense.
As you're bound to be seduced from your so-called Quest,
In future, Roland, leave the seducing to me.
Or can't I, perhaps, compete with your ladies of pleasure?

Roland
Pleasure? That was not pleasure.

Sylvie
It was. But it was not happiness.

Roland
And *you* offer me happiness?

Sylvie
You doubt that I have it to offer?

Roland
No, I don't doubt that. But my tutor always said
Happiness cannot be taken as a present.

Sylvie
Forget your tutor. This is a foreign land
Where no one will interfere with us.

Roland
No one? No *man* perhaps.

Sylvie
What do you mean by that?

Roland
Look round you, Sylvie. See the deserted port,
The ruined shacks, the slagheaps covered with lichen
And behind it all the frown and fear of the forest.
This is the Dragon's demesne.

Sylvie
Roland, how childish you are.

Roland
You think so? Look at this notice
That flaps here on the hoarding –
And this one and this one and this one.

Sylvie (*reading*)
'Wanted for Murder' . . . 'Wanted for Murder' . . . 'Wanted' –

Roland
You're reading the words wrong. Not 'for', Sylvie, 'to'!

Sylvie
'Wanted to Murder.' You're right.
But what does it mean?

Roland
It means we are on a soil where murder pays.

Sylvie
It pays in many places.

Roland
Yes, but here
The paymaster is the government – and pay-day
Is every day of the week.
The Dragon's doing, I tell you.

Sylvie
Well, if it is, *you* cannot cure it.
At the best you can cure yourself.
(*Tentatively.*)
And that only through love.

Roland
Love?

Sylvie (*stronger*)
Through me, Roland, through me.

Pause.

Roland (*quietly, as if solving a problem*)
Yes, I think you're right. (*Then with sudden decisiveness.*)
Sylvie, take this ring; I cannot wear it now,
I have failed this ring – but this ring will not fail you.

Sylvie
You mean. . . ?

Roland
Yes. Let me put it on your finger.

Sylvie
Not yet, Roland. That must be done in a church.

Roland
And where can we find a church round here?

Sylvie (*half-abstracted*)
What a strange colour. Like the blood of a child.

Roland
I repeat! Where can we find a church or a chapel here?

The **Tout** *pops up. He speaks in broken English.*

Tout
Scusa. Lady and gentleman want guide to chapel?

Roland
God! Where did this come from?

Tout
Me? Me come from sewer.
Me accredited guide – very good, very funny.
Lady and gentleman see chapel today?

Roland
Where is this chapel of yours?

Tout
Chapel not mine, chapel belong to God.
Me take you there up this road, see.
Me tell the history, very much history, cheap.

A distant bell is heard, which continues as they speak.

That chapel bell, tee-hee!
Ring-a-ling for the wedding!

Roland
What wedding?

Tout
Me not know. No, sir, nobody know.
Happy pair not come yet.

Sylvie
Roland, this is a sign.
Tell him to show us the way.

Tout
Me show you the way sure.
Beautiful lady put best foot first.
Chapel up there in forest.

Roland
In the forest?

Tout
Sure, boss. Chapel old.
Chapel in forest before forest grew.
But needs repairs now bad.
Haunted too – tee-hee!

Roland
Haunted!

Tout
Sure, boss.
Plenty of ghosts – tu-whit, tu-whoo.
Me need bonus for them ghosts.

Roland
You'll have your bonus. Only get us there quick.
Sylvie, we will exorcise these ghosts.
You know how, my dearest?

Sylvie (*heartfelt*)
I know how.

The bell continues but is gradually submerged by orchestral chapel music. The latter swell
to a definite close, leaving **Roland** *and* **Sylvie** *in the Haunted Chapel. The voices echo*
in the emptiness.

Priest (*old and tired, but kindly*)
You have the ring? Good.
Before I complete this ceremony making you man and wife
I must deliver a warning.
The original sin is in doubt.
And in these days the contempt for the individual
It is also the topical sin.
So if either of you has doubts of the holiness of marriage
Or if either of you has doubts of the other
And can conceive a time when he or she
Will think again and wish this thing undone,
Now is your time to speak.
Pause.
Good. So you have no doubts. There is one other formality.
Although there is no congregation present,
Although apart from ourselves and a few sparrows and fieldmice

The chapel is now empty, I must still put the question:
If anyone here know just cause or impediment –

He is interrupted by voices with a strange acoustic.

Blind Peter's Voice
I do!

Gavin's Voice
I do!

Father's Voice
I do!

Blind Peter's Voice
This young man who's come to you to get married
Promised me when he left, a week before I died,
As he would avenge my blindness and bring it about
How no one should go the way I went in future.
Well, has he done it? No, and he'll never do it –
Not if you splice him up to that poor simple girl
Who only dreams how he and she will be happy.

Gavin's Voice
No, Roland, my brother; Blind Peter is right.
Forget your dreams of a home. You can never be happy
If you forsake the Quest. And if you could –
Happiness is not all. You must go on –
Turn your back on this chapel, go on through the forest,
Alone, always alone, and then across the desert,
And at the other end of that desert –

Father's Voice (*very deep*)
You will find what I found, Roland.

Roland
You?

Father's Voice
You should know my voice though you never heard it.
Though you had not seen me, you know my portrait.

Roland
My father?

Father's Voice
I am still waiting to be your father.
While you malinger, you are no son of mine.

Roland (*shattered*)
Sylvie. . . .

Sylvie
I know what you want . . . Your ring.

She tries to retain self-control in making her renunciation.

There . . . Back on your finger.
Look how it glows in this darkness.

Roland (*bitterly*)
Glows? It will burn me up.

Sylvie
Roland, before we part –

Priest
This chapel is now closed. I am sorry.
Goodbye, my daughter; your way lies back,
Back by the road you came over the hopeless sea,
Back to your little house and your apple orchard
And there must you marry one of your own kind
And spray the trees in spring and raise the ladders in autumn
And spread the shining crop on the spare-room floor and –

Roland
Sylvie, before we part –

Priest
This chapel is now closed. I am sorry.
Goodbye, my son; your way lies forward,
Forward through the gibbering guile of the forest,
Forward through the silent doubt of the desert.
And here let me warn you: if in the forest
You hear any voices call from the trees,
Pay no attention, Roland, pay no attention . . .

His voice fades as forest magic grows up; out of its tangle come the voices of the birds, harsh and mechanical, speaking in a heavily stressed sing-song rhythm.

Parrot
Pretty Polly! Pretty Polly!
Who's this coming now?

Raven
Caw-caw! Caw-caw!
Who's a-walkin' in *my* forest?

Parrot
Pretty Polly! The leaves have fallen.

Raven
Caw-caw! He's walking late.

Parrot
Pretty Polly! He's looking pale.

Raven
Caw-caw! Greet him!

Parrot (*sneeringly*)
Where are you going, Roland, so fast?

Raven
Roland, running away from your past?

Both
You can't do *that*! You can't do *that*!

Parrot
Still on the road? Still on the Quest?

Raven
None can achieve it but the best.

Both
You're not the sort. You're not the sort.

Parrot
Why not stop, my dear young man?

Raven
Let heroes die as heroes can.

Both
You must *live*! *You* must *live*!

The forest music swells up as **Roland** *passes.*

Parrot
Pretty Polly! He's passed us by.

Raven
Caw-caw! The devil take him.

Parrot
Pretty Polly! The devil will.

The forest music gives place to desert music and **Roland** *is heard soliloquizing.*

Roland (*very tired*)
Oh this desert!
The forest was bad enough but this beats all.
When my tutor described it to me, it sounded strange
But now I am here, with the grit of it filling my shoes,
I find that the worst thing about it is this:

The desert is something familiar.
And with no end – no end.

The music ends.

Flat – No shape – No colour – Only here and there
A mirage of the past – something I've met before –
Figures arising from dust, repeating themselves,
Telling me things that I have no wish to remember.
Mirage . . . mirage . . . mirage. . . .

Clock Voice
Tick Tock, Tick Tock,
Tick Tock, Tick Tock. . . .

Continuing in background as the first mirage is heard.

Soak
A pretty boy – but I've given him no more lines.
He'd never guess what happens in my dream.
Look – a pull on the wire, his feet move forward.
Left Right, Left Right. . . .

He synchronizes with the **Clock Voice** *as it comes again into the foreground.*

Clock Voice
Tick Tock (etc.)

Soak
Left Right (etc.)

They withdraw to the background as the second mirage appears.

Steward
Golden days, sir, golden days.
In the desert, sir, have you noticed
One doesn't notice time?
But I thought so the moment I saw you:
You don't know where you're going.
Golden days, golden days. . . .

He synchronizes with the **Clock Voice** *and* **Soak** *– the same procedure.*

Clock Voice	Tick Tock, *etc.*
Soak	Left Right, *etc.*
Steward	Golden days, *etc.*

Neaera
. . . adagio . . . rallentendo . . .
This dossier includes your future –
You don't come out of it well.

But kiss me, Roland, kiss me.
Kiss me, kiss me. . . . (*Synchronizes.*)

Clock Voice	Tick Tock, *etc.*
Soak	Left Right, *etc.*
Steward	Golden days, *etc.*
Neaera	Kiss me, *etc.*

Sylvie
But why must you go so quickly?
Now that the sun's coming out?
You, Roland – you're no knight errant.
Your love for me will triumph, you'll come back,
Then you and I, you and I . . . (*Synchronizes.*)

Clock Voice	Tick Tock, *etc.*
Soak	Left Right, *etc.*
Steward	Golden days, *etc.*
Neaera	Kiss me, *etc.*
Sylvie	You and I, *etc.*

The five voices swell in the foreground, driving as it were at the camera, till **Roland** *can bear it no longer.*

Roland (*screaming*)
NO!

The voices break off as if cut with a knife.

Roland
Shapes of dust and fancy! Unreal voices!
But where is the voice that launched me on my road?
Where is the shape the first that I remember?
Why doesn't *she* appear – even in fancy?
It is the least she could – Mother, where are you?
Yes, you; I'm calling you – my mother who sent me forth –
It was all your doing. But for you
I who had no beliefs of my own,
I who had no will of my own,
Should not be here today pursuing
A dark tower that is only dark
Because it does not exist. And Mother!
It is only your will that drives me still
As signified in the blood-red stone
I wear on my finger under my glove
That burns me like a living weal. (*Suddenly puzzled.*)
. . . Burns me? . . . Burns me? . . . It always has –
But have I gone numb? I can feel nothing.

Off with this glove! I *can't* believe that –
The ring! The ring!
The colour is gone; the blood has gone out of it.
But that must mean . . . that means. . . .

Mother's Voice (*in a different acoustic, whispering*)
It means, my son, that I want you back.

Roland
And the Quest then?

Mother
Lapses.
On my deathbed I have changed my mind;
I am bearing now a child of stone.
He can go on the Quest. But you, Roland – come back!

A pause while **Roland** *takes in the implications.*

Roland
The ring . . . is always right.
Recall! Reprieve! A thousand years of sunshine!
And the apples will be in bloom round Sylvie's house.
Was that my mother's voice? Look at the ring.
It is as pale as death, there is no more breach of duty,
Her will is not behind me. Breach of duty?
If she is dying, *there* is the breach of duty –
Not to be there. Mother, you sent me out.
And I went out. Now that you call me back
I will come back! The desert take this ring –
It serves no further purpose!

He throws away the ring, and is startled at clink.

What was that?
It must have struck something hard. That's the first
Sound I've heard in the desert. Where did I throw that ring?
A stone? But a carved stone! Looks like a milestone.
As if the desert had any use for milestones! (*With a hysterical half-laugh.*)
How many miles to Babylon? Let's see now;
These letters are choked with sand, 'To Those . . . To Those . . .'

He deciphers the inscription, reading it aloud slowly.

'To Those Who Did Not Go Back –
Whose Bones being Nowhere, their signatue is for All Men –
Who went to their Death of their Own Free Will
Bequeathing Free Will to Others.'

The bird voices cut in, jeering.

Parrot
Pretty Polly! A tall story!

Raven
Caw-caw! And not so new!

Parrot
Pretty Polly! Unknown warriors!

Raven
Caw-caw! Nobody cares!

Parrot
'Who went to their death!' – Pretty Polly!

Raven
'Of their own free will!' – Caw-caw!

Roland
Of their own free will? It wasn't like that with me.
It was my mother pushed me to this point
And now she pulls me back. Let's see this ring –
Where's it fallen? Hm. Yes, there's no mistake,
Red no longer: my mother wants me back
And indeed it is high time; this desert has no end
Nor even any contour, the blank horizon
Retreats and yet retreats; without either rise or fall
Repeats, retreats, defeats; there is no sign of a tower –
You could see a tower for miles; there is not even a knoll,
Flatness is all – and nothing. Own free will?

He has been speaking quietly but now bursts out.

As if I Roland had ever . . . Tutors, trumpeters, women,
Old soaks and crooked stewards, everyone I have met
Has played his music on me. Own free will!
Three words not one of which I understand!
All right, Mother dear, I'm coming.

Pause.

Now . . . Where are my footsteps? Better follow them back.
Are these my footsteps? But how small they look!
Well, you're a small man, Roland – Better admit it –
You'll be still smaller now . . . But are these my footsteps?
They are so near together – and I thought
I was walking with great strides! O Roland, Roland,
You thought yourself a hero – and you walked
With little steps like that! Now you must watch
These niggling footprints all your return journey.
To underline your shame. What's shame to me

220 MAKING SCENES 3

Who never had free will? . . . 'Their own free will
Bequeathing free will to others.' Others indeed!
I begin to think my drunken friend was right
In his subjective tavern; there are no others
Apart from the projections of my mind
And, once that mind is empty, man's a desert.
(*Losing his temper.*) Others! Who are these others? Where can I find 'em?

Child's Voice (*out of the blue*)
Nowhere, Roland. Nowhere.

Roland
There! What did I say? There *are* no –

Child's Voice
You will find us if you go forward –
For you will be dead before we are born.
You will never find us if you go back –
For you will have killed us in the womb.

Roland
What! So I'm an infanticide now?

Child's Voice
Not yet. But if you go back . . .

Roland
Who said I was going back?

Child's Voice
I thought you had made up your mind.

Roland
I never make up my mind!
Didn't I say that my mother – Look, I'll leave it to chance;
Chance is as good an artiber as any.
Watch me, you unborn children. See this tiny cactus?
I will strip it leaf by leaf – let that decide –
This Year, Next Year, Eena-Meena – you know the game, *you* unborn
  children.
Now.

He counts in regular time, but with growing tension, as he picks off the leaves.

Forward – back; forward – back; forward – back – forward;
Back – forward; back – forward; back – forward – back;
Forward – back; forward – back; forward – back – forward;
Back – forward; back – forward; back – forward – BACK.
There! The voice of chance. The oracle of the cactus.

Back! Back! That's what the cactus says.
But I'm . . .

He holds the suspense, then with decision.

. . going forward, children!
Did you think that I'd let a cactus dictate to me?
Mother, don't pull on the string; you must die alone.
Forgive me, dear, but – I tell you I'm going forward.
Forward, Roland . . . into the empty desert,
Where all is flat and colourless and silent.

He pauses; the orchestra creeps in with a heartbeat rhythm.

Silent? . . . Then what's this?
Something new! A *sound!* But a sound of what?
Don't say that it's my heart! Why, Roland you poor fool,
Who would think you had one? You must be afraid;
It is fear reveals the heart.

Heartbeat louder.

Aha, you piece of clockwork –
Trying to have your little say while you can!
Before your wheels run down here in the empty desert.

Sudden chord; the heartbeat continues.

Empty? . . . Where have those mountains come from?
Closing round in a ring, humpbacked horrors
That want to be in at the death. And where's the horizon?
A moment ago this was level. What's the game?
A confidence trick? A trap? I am cooped in.
A circle of ugly cliffs – a lobster-pot of rock!
Silence, my stupid heart! This looks like . . . looks like what?
This looks like the great circus in Ancient Rome,
Only there is no audience – and no lions.
(*Suddenly noticing.*) No audience?

Chord; heartbeat behind – and steadily increasing.

No audience! Why, that's Gavin on top of that peak!
And Michael and Denis and Henry and Roger and John!
And men that I've never seen – in outlandish clothes,
Some of them even in armour. And there's Blind Peter –
With sight in his eyes, for he's pointing –
And my father too – I remember him from the album –
And my tutor – he must be dead – looking graver than ever
And – well – to the front of course – my dear old Sergeant-Trumpeter.

Figure in the music; the succeeding voices, other than **Roland**'s *own, sound as if coming from somewhere far-off and above.*

Sergeant-Trumpeter
Roland! Hold the note at the end.

Gavin
Be ready, old boy. This is it!

Blind Peter
Strike a good blow to avenge Blind Peter.

Father
Your heritage, my son. You were born to fight and –

Roland
Fight? Fight whom? This circus has no lions.

Tutor
No lions, Roland? Have you forgotten your lessons?
I never mentioned lions; it was a dragon –
And only that for lack of a better name.

Roland
Yes, yes, dragon of course – but you told me, my good tutor,
The Dragon would not appear until I came to the Tower
And until I had blown my blast – Well, there is no tower!

Gavin
That fooled *me*, Roland my brother.

Father
Look over there, Roland my son.

Roland
Where? . . . Oh *that* little thing?
Like a wart coming out of the ground!

Father
It's growing, Roland, it's growing.

Tutor
You should recognize it from my lectures.

Blind Peter
That's the joker all right.

Gavin
The tower! The Dark Tower!

Sergeant-Trumpeter
Quick now, my lad. Unsling your trumpet.

Roland
But –

Father
It's growing, my son; waste no time.

Roland
It's growing; yes, it's growing.

Child's Voice
Growing! Ohh! Look at it.
Strike a good blow for us unborn children.

Mother (*closer than the rest*)
And strike a blow for all dead mothers.

Gavin
Jump to it, Roland.

Father
Waste no time.

Sergeant-Trumpeter
Remember that challenge call.
Blow it the way I taught you.

Roland (*beginning quiet but resolute and building*)
Yes, dear friends, I will blow it the way you taught me.
I, Roland, the black sheep, the unbeliever –
Who never did anything of his own free will –
Will do this now to bequeath free will to others.

Fade out.

Ahoy there, tower, Dark Tower, you're getting big,
Your shadow is cold upon me. What of that?
And you, you Dragon, or whatever you are
Who make men beasts, come out – here is a man;
Come out and do your worst.

The heartbeat, having reached its crescendo, ends clean.

Roland (*restrained, in the sudden silence*)
Wrist be steady
As I raise the trumpet so – now fill my lungs –

The Challenge Call rings out; the Sergeant-Trumpeter speaks as the last long note is reached.

Sergeant-Trumpeter
Good lad, Roland. Hold that note at the end.

The trumpet holds it, enriched and endorsed by the orchestra. They come to a full close.

If we do not feed the Dragon with blood, what happens?

Jim Mulligan talks to Michael Quinn, producer of The Dark Tower *for BBC Belfast*

The year after World War II ended, *The Dark Tower*, was broadcast for the first time, with original music composed by Benjamin Britten. Louis MacNeice was to direct the play four times in all, once as a stage production. Since then the play has generally been considered quintessential radio drama. It is not surprising, therefore, that Michael Quinn, a producer for BBC Belfast, chose the play as part of BBC's epic undertaking *Towards the Millennium*, a decade-by-decade overview of the most significant achievements in the arts of the twentieth century.

'There are moments in *The Dark Tower* when you feel the poetic and the dramatic jarring. It can be obscure but if it connects with people it is precisely because it is heightened by the poetry. When I was directing the play, actors would ask me: "What does it mean?" I think a more pertinent question is: "What does it make you feel?" It's a provocative play. It makes you think, but the conduit is through your heart. It's difficult to talk about Louis MacNeice without sounding pretentious, because his work is drenched with allusions and he is very erudite, but a simple way of looking on it is to see the play as a quest for self. That is why it is so potent.'

The play was written in response to the events of World War II. It seems clear that Louis MacNeice has the rise of fascism in Germany in mind when Blind Peter says: 'Everything went sour; people's mouths and eyes changed their look overnight – and the government changed too – and as for me I woke up feeling different and, when I looked in the mirror that first morning, the mirror said, "Informer"!' What is extraordinary is how little things have changed.

'Those phantoms of tradition and authority – your country needs you – are imperatives that are still placed on people to make them do something they would rather not do: to kill people or risk being killed themselves. In *The Dark Tower* it is almost as if there is a force outside of Roland determining that he will sacrifice himself. The mother's role is crucial. It seems incredible that she should send seven sons to their death, and yet mothers have been waving their sons off as they have gone to many wars in the fifty years since this play was written. Blind Peter sorrowed for his daughter's death but she didn't for the deaths of her sons. The only way she could retain her sanity was to take refuge in duty, a terrible word, and honour is worse.'

The Tutor, an avuncular character who would much rather do research than teach says: 'We had a word, honour, but it is obsolete.' This is a strange comment when everything that drives the characters, the burden they carry is, precisely, honour, or at best duty. In Roland he finds a student who is interested in learning and asks questions but he has to send him off to make his sacrifice. The Mother sees Roland as different from her other sons but she still tries to bind him to his duty with the ring she gives him.

'Several times in the play she lists the names of the sons she has sacrificed. It is a litany that is the same as the list of names on any war memorial. In her mouth, it becomes a corrupt mantra. Those dead names place their obligation on the living. The blood sacrifice is the most potent guarantee of a sense of continuity and it is only when someone says, "I refuse to spill the blood to water the argument", that the argument or tradition withers.'

The debate about free will is central to *The Dark Tower*. Roland is sent on his quest by his mother. He vacillates and turns back. By this time, the ring his mother gave him is cold as if she has withdrawn her involvement, so that it seems he is free. He then chooses to face the evil of the Dark Tower and the terror of the dragon. It is almost as if there is a force directing him even greater than tradition, honour and duty. One of the subtleties of the play is that the Soak is the puppet master who is pulling the strings, the writer who is creating the part of Roland. We are into a labyrinth where Louis MacNeice might be the Soak or Roland might be acting freely or the Mother might be controlling events.

'I think Roland realizes that people are not defined by their tradition but by a multiplicity of things: sexuality, gender, family, geography, a sense of who you are in relation to other people. In the end he recognizes that the Dark Tower is dark only because it doesn't exist. All wars feed the dragon with blood sacrifices; it is the only way to keep back the wave of evil that is in the Dark Tower. But if we do not feed the dragon with blood what happens? Does evil flood the world? I think Louis MacNeice is presenting us with an unresolved problem. But one of the lines that rings true for me is: "To be a human being, people agree, is difficult." When World War II broke out, Louis MacNeice was in the USA and his friend Graham Sheppard, who was in the navy, was killed while on convoy escort. MacNeice applied to join the navy but was turned down on medical grounds and then returned to fight the war on the propaganda front with the BBC. It makes you wonder what his attitude is to those who answer the call of duty. I have a feeling he never got over the guilt of escaping death. It is possible that he actually approved of Roland going out to fight the dragon.'

Michael Quinn is Radio Drama Producer, BBC Northern Ireland. His production of *The Dark Tower* is the first radio broadcast of the play for over twenty years.

Louis MacNeice (1907–63) was born in Belfast. A friend of W H Auden and Stephen Spender, he was a poet, dramatist and broadcaster. His *Collected Poems* are published by Faber and Faber.

The Dark Tower

Production Notes

Setting and staging
The play lends itself to a vast group spectacle with changing landscapes.

Sound plays a crucial part in suggesting the locations – the Sea of Doubt, the ghost towns of history, the 'desert of dried up hopes', and the Dark Tower itself. There is the potential to create interesting effects with sound, voice and music, if led by the rich language of the piece. For instance:

    The sea today is timeless
    The sea today is drums and fifes . . .
    The sea today is broken bottles . . .

There is a dream-like quality to the play that might be reflected in the **lighting and costume design**. It is also important to decide what the symbols represent: the cavern, the parrot, and the clock; and to what degree the production might be influenced by political resonances.

Casting
It is worth considering using puppets or masks. The mother and the teacher, for example, might be represented symbolically. There are 22 parts, some of which might be doubled (for a minimum cast of around twelve). It is ideal for a cast with a wide age range who can do justice to the poetic language and physical demands of the piece.

Questions

1. What is the dragon and what is the Dark Tower? (What do they repesent?)

2. What is the stone baby?

3. What ideals are at stake? Should they be matters of life and death?

4. Are Roland's ideals his own or have they been handed down? How would the answer to this affect his behaviour?

5. Roland blows his trumpet to give free will to others, yet the last line is traditional. What has his quest achieved? Will it start again? Will there be a need for it to start again in the future?

Exercises

1. Imagine each character has a symbolic function – e.g. Blind Peter as Wilful Ignorance; Sylvie as Pacifist; the Trumpeter as Subservience – and create a simple drama without words (i.e. in dance, mime) exploring the various elements of the story.

2.   Select scenes and play them out while creating alternate subtexts for the characters (i.e. through improvisation).

3.   Re-create the story without words but through sounds, either musical or 'abstract', created by individuals and/or groups. Combine this work with the results achieved in exercises 1 and 2.

4.   In groups, create four 'still images', abstract or naturalistic, to depict the main elements or characters of the play. For instance, the Mother as part of a machine which creates 'War Fodder'.

5.   Animate the images created in 4. For example, to the background of one line, repeated by the group, add sound effects, etc.

6.   Experiment with more than one person playing Roland, and setting some of the longer sections of text to song, or to 'background' sounds created by the group.

7.   Explore the significance of numbers in the play. For instance, Roland is the seventh son of the seventh generation. Blind Peter must be 70. Had Roland's father lived, he would be 75.

Suzy Graham-Adriani
Director/Producer for BT National Connections